Astrological Cook-Book

Astrological Cook~Book

Eileen Deacon

Frederick Muller Limited · London

First published in Great Britain 1977
by Frederick Muller Limited, London, NW2 6LE.

Copyright © Eileen Deacon, 1977

ISBN 0 584 10204 6

British Library Cataloguing in Publication Data

Deacon, Eileen

    Astrological cook-book.
    1. Cookery   2. Astrology
    I. Title
    641.5   TX652

ISBN 0 584 10204 6

Printed in Great Britain by offset lithography
by Billing & Sons Limited
Guildford, London & Worcester

Contents

Introduction

There really isn't much fun in cooking unless it is designed to suit the palates of those for whom it is intended. That should be obvious, but so often it isn't – not even to the cook. What turns people off the chore of cooking – or rather makes what should be a pleasurable art into a chore – is, as often as not, lack of response or appreciation towards what has been, oh, so carefully prepared, and often at no small cost. "I might as well have put the dog's dinner in front of them for all the notice they took," says one hostess who has sweated for hours in the kitchen.

But how often does that same hostess ever bother to find out what her prospective guests like and dislike? Probably never at all: she just whips something up and hopes for the best. And all too often the male guest who loathes kidneys is silently revolted by the *rinones Herez*, whilst his wife, who dislikes all shell-fish, desperately tries to push the prawns under a lettuce leaf and hopes no one will notice she hasn't eaten them.

Now suppose instead the hostess not only rings up guests a few days beforehand and asks them what are their likes and dislikes in food, thus eliminating all possible chance of a culinary clanger, but also poses the question: "Under what sign of the zodiac were you born?"

Immediately the prospective guests are relieved and flattered to know that their likes and dislikes are being taken care of. And interest in the whole idea of the dinner is stimulated by the astrological inquiry. It is a fact that today most people, even if they don't take an interest in astrology, know what signs they were born under. If not, it isn't very difficult for them to find out, assuming they know their birth dates. But, of course, they will ask, "Why do you want to know?" and it is in the answer to that question that the hostess can, if she wishes, invest the whole dinner-to-be in a kind of romantic ambiance that makes her task more rewarding. She knows instinctively that she has aroused her guest's curiosity and that from now on her dinner will be a talking point. She is on her mettle, for it is essential that the dinner succeeds.

The answer to the question however is really quite simply, that there are very many good reasons why one should cook by the stars and according to the particular sign of the zodiac one was born under. Some people may scoff at this as foolish superstition. I will reply to these doubters shortly. Meanwhile I can sense that some of you will be raising the objection that as most of the guests will be born under different signs of the zodiac, how ever can you possibly cater for them all except at enormous cost and a tremendous amount of work preparing alternative dishes.

First of all, let it be admitted that probably the ideal situation in which to pose this astrological query is when you have just one guest, especially if he (or even she) is romantically-minded. However, while there are 12 signs of the zodiac these can be broken up into groups of 3 and 4 who to a very large extent share the same food tastes. So it is possible in some cases to cope quite easily with, say 2, or even 4 guests. But, if you should be planning a large party with a buffet supper, then I suggest, providing you have got the details of all the guests' zodiacal signs, you can lay out a table with snacks for Aries grouped under a label and those for Gemini, Taurus etc. similarly indicated.

What indeed could look more attractive, or arouse more interest than a round table set out with the signs of the zodiac arranged clockwise and dishes placed against each?

But, argue the doubters, this is all great fun, maybe, even a good party gimmick, but what are your reasons for saying one can cook by the stars. And haven't you got to study astrology to work all this out?

It is perfectly true that it greatly helps if you have studied astrology and continue to do so, because once you start cooking by the stars (or eating by the stars, if you don't yourself do the cooking), there is almost no limit to the extent you can experiment, adapt and improve. But it is not essential to be an astrologer; nor is deep study vital.

The first answer, or reason for the practice of cooking by the stars is that statistics show that people born under different signs of the zodiac differ in their tastes and equally in their health tendencies. Thus, there is a positive link between astrology, health, diet and food likes and dislikes.

Not all of these statistics have been compiled by astrologers. Some of them have been worked out by scientists who have total disbelief in astrology, but who nevertheless admit they are baffled by what the statistics show. The most impressive of these statistical experiments, and certainly the most objective in that the scientist carrying them out was originally hostile to astrology, are those of Michel Gauquelin, of the University of Paris. He set out to examine astrologers' claims about the influence of the planets, collecting the birth dates of more than a thousand doctors. He was astounded to discover that the planets Mars and Saturn were in a dominant position in the doctors' birth charts, positions which astrologers have for years insisted denote the talents of potential doctors.

It is important first of all to appreciate that there is a great deal of difference between what one might call "newspaper astrology" and the more scientific approach of trained astrologers. Indeed, the latter deplore what they call the bogus fortune-telling of the media. What, however, cannot be denied is that people born under, say, Sagittarius, Gemini or Taurus, are, broadly speaking, very alike the characters which astrologers claim for them. And, more important, further research shows that their health tendencies and food likes and dislikes also tally.

Of course, to get an absolutely exact picture for an individual one needs to know not merely what sign he (or she) was born under, but the actual date and time to the nearest minute of birth. If you wish, you can pursue the suggestions in this book further by getting such an exact picture by having your horoscope cast. But experience has shown that for health and dietary purposes a very accurate picture can be obtained from merely knowing the sign of the zodiac alone. And it is that we are concerned with here.

The first thing to look at is health trends. If you wish to check what astrology says with what your own health tells you, this should not be very difficult. You will be surprised how accurate the astrologers are on this score. For example, the astrologers tell us that different planets exercise an influence over different organs of the body. Thus, those born under the sign of Virgo are liable to suffer from intestinal and digestive ailments, while those who are Librans, which is ruled by Venus, have a sweet tooth, which can be encouraged within limits, but should avoid too rich a diet. They tend to suffer from backache and kidney trouble. Sagittarians are prone to nervous exhaustion and rheumatism.

In some instances the health trends show a direct link with a suitable diet. Those born under the sign of Taurus suffer a great deal from digestive troubles and from not eating the right food. They are advised to avoid too many sweet things and to watch their diet, especially in later life. Gemini people tend to be erratic in their eating habits, to skip meals and eat very little for days, even weeks, and then to indulge in an orgy of feasting.

Pisceans have a passion for fish, not surprising in view of their particular sign of the zodiac. But many of them suffer from this because they also have a hidden allergy for certain fish dishes, usually the more exotic fish, oysters and some shellfish particularly.

What this book aims to do is to provide a separate chapter for each sign of the zodiac, giving in each a concise summary of what foods are most suitable, giving reasons why and explaining what should be avoided. This will be followed by a list of five recipes applicable for each sign and, to round it all off, a menu for one set dinner for each sign. You may not want to keep slavishly to what astrology tells you to do, but I think that anyone with a sense of fun or a love of trying something new, would agree that a surprise birthday dinner for your Capricornian husband, or the Aquarian girl friend, as the case may be, is something that might well produce a bonus!

But before you start turning to the various chapters some guidance apart from the foregoing may be of interest to those who always like to know the whys and wherefores. The theory that there are links between the stars and the human organs has been held for centuries by the gypsies and they have long believed that each person's horoscope sign shows how one should watch one's health. The gypsies have linked these theories with their own philosophy of herbal medicine and even prescribe herbs, fruit and vegetables for each sign of the zodiac.

Modern astrologers and even some homeopathic doctors who have themselves made a study of this ancient lore have together come to the conclusion that experiment proves that much of it is scientifically true. One doesn't know how or why this is, but one has only to look at the influence of the moon on various aspects of life on earth to see that stellar influences are not so fanciful as might at first be thought.

There are, of course, exceptions to every rule, but, broadly speaking, statistics show that those born under the various signs do tend to suffer from the ailments specified by the astrologers e.g. Aquarians are prone to injury of legs and ankles and suffer from nervous complaints and poor circulation. However, in this cookery book we shall only concentrate on those health trends which have a distinct and direct bearing on what one should and should not eat – e.g. Capricornians need to watch their liver and Arians tend to have stomach and kidney trouble.

Madame de Chrapowicki, a Polish scientist, puts it like this: "the major keynote of a body relates to that particular quality and vibratory rhythm which was dominant in the atmosphere at the exact time of birth and which will influence and even control all other vibrations during that body's life span."

Out of all this has developed the theory of astro-biochemistry, which is based on a scientific study of the relationship between astrology and biochemistry. One of the main findings of this relationship has been that there is a link between the twelve signs of the zodiac and the twelve mineral elements – the twelve tissue salts which are to be found in the formation of the human body.

The theory is that everyone has a "birth salt", that is to say the salt allocated to the sign under which one is born. And everyone tends to use up this salt more than any of the others. Thus we all have a mineral in which we are likely to be deficient. For example, those born under Aries are liable to be deficient in phosphate of potassium, those under Leo will tend to lack magnesium phosphate. From these details, plus those already gleaned for health trends under the different signs of the zodiac, it is possible to prescribe in general terms what foods are beneficial and which are not. Apart from this it is also possible to bring homeopathic medicine to bear on the "astrological evidence": certain herbs suit certain signs of the zodiac. There are biochemic and homeopathic remedies for each sign.

What modern astrologers have done, in collaboration with scientists and homeopathic doctors, is to compile a very simple chart which gives the birth salt of each sign of the zodiac together with scientifically accurate recommendations as to how to make good the salt deficiency not only in diet, but in chemicals, herbs, fruit, vegetables etc. And it is on these findings that this Astrological Cook Book has been based.

Like all things and especially all theories, one has to use moderation and commonsense. Those who take this advice and wish to pursue it further may not only wish to study astrology and astro-biochemistry, but have their horoscope cast so that the findings of the doctors and scientists may be applied with even greater accuracy. I am sure that, if they have time, they will find further study surprisingly rewarding.

On the other hand, as a word of warning, I should add that as far as food and diet is concerned, even with a personal horoscope they will have to play it by ear: in other words, compare the horoscopic findings and suggestions with their own experience. On no account worry too much about the ailments which, according to your sign of the zodiac, you may be prone. Take note of them, ask yourself whether they apply to you. But remember that you may not actually suffer from those ailments yet, but you might in future. It may be that you are not so deficient in your birth salt as most of your zodiac sign.

Another point to remember is that those of you who are born on the cusp – i.e. born right at the end of one sign of the zodiac, or right at the beginning – may well share some of the characteristics of the sign nearest to your own. If, for example, you were born on 18 February, you will probably have some of the characteristics of Pisces as well as of Aquarius. In this instance you should certainly have a look at the recipes for *both* signs.

Some of you, probably a majority, will want to try out these suggestions with tongue in cheek, looking upon it as a rather amusing exercise, but possibly only trying out the recipes in this book. To you I would say that I am certainly not pretending you could or should live on the five exercises provided for each sign. The book is intended for those of you who are imaginative and practical enough to use the basic advice contained in each chapter to work out some new recipes and menus for yourselves. If you study the five recipes under each sign carefully, you will see that they can easily be adapted into other dishes, that what may seem to be a mere hors d'oeuvre can be turned into a meal in itself, or that some main courses can be reduced to the size of a snack.

For those of you prepared to follow up the book this far I should like to make the point that, broadly speaking, one should group those with similar tastes and needs (often rather a different thing from tastes!) NOT under the Air, Fire, Water and Earth Signs, as some people tend to do, but under those with similar birth salts.

The following groups not only more or less share similar tastes, but also have similar dietary needs:

1 Aquarius, Libra and Taurus (a sodium group);
2 Capricorn, Cancer and Scorpio (a calcium group);
3 Aries, Gemini and Virgo (a potassium group).

Not so easy to place in a group and much more individualistic are Leo, Pisces and Sagittarius. There are some astrologers who try to fit them into groupings with other signs of the zodiac, but this never really works and sometimes is quite disastrous.

I imagine that many of you, while not particularly worrying about what suits yourselves, will be paying more attention to the ideas submitted for your friends, relatives or guests under other signs.

Whether or not you are for or against astrology, the real fun in astrological cooking is doing things for other people. It need not be cranky and, whatever else happens, you can be sure your dinner party will be a talking point.

If you do not become the hostess with the mostest, then you will be well on the way to becoming the hostess who gets the reputation for making eating out fun. And to the minority who may be violently opposed to astrology as distinct from just indifferently dubious, I can only say, "Well, you haven't got to believe it, or support astrology. After all, this is essentially a book about food and cooking, not about the stars."

Human nature being what it is, any prospective guest, and especially any newly acquired friend of the opposite sex, will be hugely flattered at the thought that you have taken the trouble not only to discover his or her birthday date, but to plan out a menu to fit this. It will not matter all that much whether this is followed up by a dinner which you cook yourself, or one which you order specially at the restaurant of your choice: the overall effect should be the same.

However, in an imperfect world and working solely on signs of the zodiac and not on individually worked out horoscopes, you should be warned that to a certain extent there is an element of hit-and-miss in this game. But the "hits" should far outnumber the misses because the vital element in this astrological cookery is that of the birth salt which is covered by the whole month period of the zodiac sign.

From one point of view it is probably easier and safer to plan an astrological meal at home than to risk one out at a restaurant. I have suggested a birthday menu with appropriate wines and liqueurs for each zodiacal sign. But it could well be that "inside information" on your guest will cause you to want to make a substitution somewhere in the menu. Or it may be you are a little uncertain about one or two of the more exotic dishes suggested. In this case it will be best to choose a substitute dish from one of those listed among the recipes for that sign, or alternatively you can make a swop for one of the dishes suggested or hinted at in the preface to that sign.

If I seem to be labouring the point here, it is because I am genuinely concerned to point out the pitfalls. Having made up your mind to go "astrological", you might as well aim at perfection. If you decide to go flat out for one of the meals I have suggested for a birthday menu, I suggest you choose your restaurant very carefully indeed.

You might be lucky in that a restaurant you know has all the items quoted on its own menu. But this may not always be easy, especially if you live in the country. However, despite all talk of falling-off in standards, it is probably true to say that the standards of cooking everywhere in the world are much higher today in the depths of the country than ever they were in the past.

Almost certainly you should be able to find a restaurant within ten miles radius anywhere in Britain and certainly in Europe, where you will find a helpful restauranteur who, if consulted and given enough advance notice, will plan a special menu for you. But give him time – if possible two or three days' notice – for your planned birthday treat.

In one sense we are all tending to be more international and less insular in our food tastes. But there will always be some who are conditioned by the habits and tastes acquired in the country in which they were born. Take this into account when planning your menu and this applies particularly to the subject of drink.

With some signs of the zodiac the choice of drinks can make or mar an evening out. An appendix on the subject at the end of this book can be consulted for advice on a subject that is rather more individualistic than astrological. If you reckon you are knowledgeable on wines and what goes with which, by all means skip the appendix. On the other hand it might just provide a new idea even for someone who has made a study of the subject. Not that I can promise you an astrological cocktail!

Careful study of the suggestions made under your own sign will help to point the way to the type of regular meals which you could well adopt. I am now talking of the every day meal rather than the special occasion. You will find that from a health point of view over a long period it will be enormously beneficial if you bear in mind the do's and don'ts for your own sign of the zodiac. This has been borne out by homeopathic research.

Many who have tried to follow the rules laid down for astrological eating have been amazed to find that their health has actually benefited from doing so. This is particularly the case when they have been suffering from digestive troubles, or other ailments, not least from those linked with rheumatism.

You will see that the rules are not really irksome. They are designed to guide, to point the way, to be constructive, not to set out a long list of do's or don'ts. In fact, in these twelve astrological pointers to what you should eat all are given a fairly wide range of choices. You should, however, pay special attention to any of the vegetables, fruits, herbs etc. recommended which you may never before have eaten.

From the lists given you should be able to work out many additional recipes for yourselves. As to the recipes, I have tried to bear in mind several points that are not usually included in cookery books. It is still assumed that women do most of the cooking. In fact, each year the number of men who can cook reasonably well is increasing all the time. Probably today there are very many married couples who find it is essential to share the duties of cooking – his turn tonight, hers tomorrow!

I have no doubt that men can follow a cook-book just as well as women, but I have tried to make the instructions simple and clear and to avoid being complicated and dogmatic. I also hope that this policy will be appreciated by many women who often have to dash back from an office or shop to prepare a special meal. The last thing they want is to waste time looking backwards and forwards from the stove or oven to the cookery book which, far, far too often, is the nerve-biting state of affairs created by relying on a book to get you that special meal on time.

The aim of these recipes is to try not to make even the trickiest of them too complicated for the cook in a hurry, or for the man who suddenly decides to cast caution to the winds and for the first time in his life tries to cook a birthday meal to win over his girl.

Most of the recipes are based on easily obtainable ingredients. Partridges are not easily found today even in season, it is perfectly true. On the other hand, providing you can find your partridge, you are given a simple recipe for serving one, devoid of any of the extras and tarted-up trimmings which so often go with this bird. You will find that your simple dish stands up to any of those of the *cordon bleu* cooks.

Even some of the more exotic sounding sweets are really very easy to produce. The lesson here is not to waste time on puddings and tarts, which all mean extra cooking and sometimes the making of pastry. Thus you are able to concentrate on your main dish and can choose an easily prepared, but still somewhat glamorous-looking sweet, and it is all there in the refrigerator ready to be served. Only with a few types such as Librans is it necessary to pay the same attention to a sweet as you would to a main course.

I have so often found that most cookery books fail by being too categorical. Cookery, like writing, calls for inspiration. If it was just a matter of slavishly following the instructions of a recipe, the highly-paid chef would not exist. The real cook is an artist, one who cannot be hemmed in by rigid rules, and, above all, one who relies first and foremost on his sense of smell, taste and sight. Without having all his talents in these three senses, he might as well throw away any cookery book.

For one person an hour's cooking may be just right, for another it may need half an hour more. You may want to hurl in the extra teaspoonful of this herb, or that. If you feel like it, do just that. But taste and smell before acting. I give measurements in simple approximations – glassfuls rather than quarter pints, tablespoons or teaspoons rather than so many ounces of fractions or an ounce in some instances.

Only in very few cases have I positively given any indication of the exact setting for your oven, be it gas or electric, and indeed I have allowed for the fact that you may be cooking on equipment which does not offer any carefully regulated settings. I have tended to use the words "moderate" or "low", or similar phraseology for ovens and only occasionally suggested a definite setting. This is done purely as a guide; it is then up to you to act as you see fit.

So very many cookery recipes fail by falling into the error of giving too precise instructions. Because of this I tend to offer a time range for cooking rather than a precise number of minutes – e.g. 5–7 minutes, or 20–30 minutes.

One should never be too precise in cooking. Very rarely can anyone expect always to cook the same meal exactly the same way. Sometimes it will be better, sometimes worse, no matter how many times you do it. But this is not quite so depressing as it sounds. Usually, you will find, when there is the inspiration or incentive to do really well, the cook will live up to the occasion. But unwelcome guests may fare less well!

If you want some reassurance that these ideas and recipes are not only the work of apprentice sorcerers and some female muttering incantations over a bubbling pot, like one of Macbeth's witches, let me just remind you that the discovery of the link between the twelve signs of the zodiac and the mineral elements (or birth salts) was made by a qualified doctor, Dr. George W. Carey, M.D. And yet another doctor, Dr. James B. Williamson, M.B., B.S., M.R.C.S., M.F.Hom., who supports the gypsy methods of health treatment (methods which are based on astrology) has this to say: "I have no hesitation in advising people to follow the Romany gypsy way to healing, health and happiness."

For this very reason I have also included at the end of the book an astrological chart for your kitchen and medical chest. This is, in effect, a quick reference summary of the birth salts and health tendencies of each sign of the zodiac, with some tips which may be as valuable for your own diet as for your general health.

Eileen Deacon

Recipes For Aries

21 March — 20 April

Aries is the first sign of the zodiac. Those who are born in this period are sometimes liable to suffer from headaches, brain fatigue and neuralgia, while from a dietary point of view they may have stomach and kidney ailments. On the whole they are healthy and vigorous individuals, but they are apt to develop stomach ailments through being easily angered.

Aries' birth salt is potassium phosphate and it is worth noting in connection with the tendency towards brain fatigue that potassium phosphate actually creates the grey matter of the brain when it combines with albumen and oxygen. Thus a deficiency in this salt can lead to mental tiredness and even irritability. Foods which are rich in potassium phosphate are, first and foremost, the tomato, secondly, red beet, and in addition celery, lemons, grapefruit, parsnips and apples.

The Aries-type usually likes what is straightforward and simple in food. Occasionally they have a tendency towards nibbling and to check this most of them need to have a fairly substantial breakfast and a low-calorie diet. Asparagus, cauliflower, cabbage, carrots and strawberries are not only beneficial for Aries people, but usually popular with them.

It is a fairly safe rule that this type should not be given excessively rich dishes, or anything that tends to put on weight. A few Aries-types are apt to be fanatics on keeping fit and maintaining a strict diet.

18

Aries man can be demanding: he usually likes thick, juicy steaks. Male and female are red meat eaters, preferring roasts and grills to any tarted-up variations.

Aries Salad

Enough for 2 persons

Ingredients: 1 medium-sized crisp eating apple; a few sprigs of watercress; 1 heart of fresh celery; 1 medium-sized tomato; quarter of firm cabbage heart; 3 tablespoons of sunflower seed oil; 1 tablespoon of cider vinegar; juice of half a small lemon; salt and black ground pepper to taste.

Method: Mix oil, vinegar, lemon juice, seasoning well together in salad bowl. Roughly grate cabbage, slice celery fairly thinly; cut apple into small cubes, mix thoroughly together, place in salad dressing and mix well. Garnish with segments of tomatoes and sprigs of watercress.

Prawns and Asparagus in White Sauce

Enough for 2 persons, or even 3 if used as a small hors d'oeuvre

Ingredients: 6 oz. peeled frozen prawns (allow to defreeze); 1 small tin of tips and spears of asparagus (or fresh asparagus if in season); pinch of grated nutmeg; pinch of ground mace; 2 oz. butter or margarine; 1 oz. plain flour; ¾ pint of milk; 2 tablespoons of cream; paprika.

Method: Place prawns and drained asparagus in layers in oven-proof dish; put in moderately heated oven, covering with foil. Melt butter in medium-sized saucepan, take off the heat and add flour; cook for 2 minutes, stirring all the time. Then take off the heat. Meanwhile heat milk and pour slowly into butter and flour, while stirring. Replace on heat, still stirring and slowly bring to boil and cook for 4–5 minutes. Add seasoning and cream. Remove prawns and asparagus from oven, then pour sauce over them and sprinkle with paprika. Serve while hot. A little of the asparagus liquid from the tin may be added to the sauce, if desired.

Vegetable Soup

Enough for 2–3 persons

Ingredients: 2 tablespoons of sunflower seed oil; 1 medium-sized carrot; 1 tablespoon pearl barley; 1 stick of celery; parmesan cheese; 1 medium-size turnip; 1 medium-size tomato; bouquet of mixed herbs – thyme, parsley, bayleaf – in piece of muslin, tied with cotton; 1 medium-size onion; 1½ pints of stock or beef cube; seasoning.

Method: Chop onion roughly and lightly brown for a few minutes in a saucepan on a medium heat. Dice carrots, turnip, celery, tomato and mix with onion; add stock and bouquet and pearl barley. Bring to boil, then simmer for ¾ hour. Remove bouquet and serve with parmesan cheese.

Grilled Fillet of Steak on Croutons, Garnished with Mushrooms, Tomatoes and Carrots

Enough for 3 persons

Ingredients: 3 pieces of fillet steak about 2 inches thick; ½ lb. carrots; ½ lb. button mushrooms; 2 oz. butter; 3 tomatoes; 3 rounds of white bread the size of steaks, ½ inch thick.

Method: Trim steak, if necessary, and brush with olive oil before grilling. Peel and cut carrots lengthwise and cook in salted water. Wash and dry mushrooms: do not peel, but cut off excessive stalks. Make a cross with a knife on each tomato at the opposite end to the stalks; then place under the grill 5 minutes before you start to grill steaks, putting a little melted butter on each tomato. Cook tomatoes until tender, but still firm. Grill the steaks on each side for 6 minutes. Fry bread on both sides in butter until brown and crisp; then place croutons on hot dishes with steaks on top of each and garnish with tomatoes, mushrooms and carrots; sprinkle with chopped parsley. Serve at once very hot.

Marshmallow Delight

Enough for 2–3 persons

Ingredients: 9 marshmallows; ½ lb. raspberries; 1 small tin of pineapple rings; 1 small carton of double cream; juice of half a lemon; ½ pint fresh orange jelly (made from oranges); 1 level dessertspoon of gelatine.

Method: Cut 6 of the marshmallows into small pieces. Put on one side 4 raspberries; cut pineapple into small pieces; whisk cream. Place a layer of raspberries in a glass dish, or sundae glasses, sprinkling with lemon and orange juices. Then add a layer of marshmallow, and, finally, a layer of pineapple, sprinkling each layer with the lemon juice. Dissolve a little gelatine in a little hot water over a low heat until completely transparent, adding to remaining orange juice. Allow almost to set and then pour over ingredients in the glass dishes. Place in the refrigerator until set. Top with the whipped cream and decorate with remaining marshmallows cut into halves and raspberries, and serve.

The Birthday Menu

Jellied consommé with ice cube

Steak flambé with green salad
and new potatoes

Strawberries in red wine

Wine: Château Cantermerle (a red Médoc)

NB Aries-types nearly always like coffee,
but do not so often enjoy liqueurs.

The Birthday Menu

The cheapest and quickest method of turning out a jellied consommé at short notice is to buy a tin of consommé of a good brand and leave in the refrigerator for 12 hours to set. Place ice cubes in a soup bowl, put the jellied consommé on top of the cubes and serve at once. For the steak flambé buy two fillet steaks about two inches thick; wipe with a damp cloth. Grill the steaks on each side for 5–6 minutes. Heat 2 tablespoons of brandy in a very small saucepan; remove the steaks from the grill and place on a very hot dish. Pour the hot brandy over them and light with a match. Serve immediately. Prepare green salad in the usual way, with oil, vinegar, salt and pepper to taste. Place 1 lb. of new potatoes in boiling salt water with a squeeze of lemon juice, 1 lump of sugar and mint: cook until tender.

Strawberries in red wine: remove the husks from 1 lb. of strawberries and gently wipe with a damp cloth. Place in a glass dish, sprinkle all over with a level tablespoon of castor sugar and pour over a small glass of red wine. Allow to stand in a refrigerator for one hour.

Recipes For Taurus

21 April — 20 May

Generally speaking, it is a pleasure to cater for Taureans because they have the biggest appetites of any sign of the zodiac and particularly love interesting food. They enjoy good health as a rule and have a good digestion, being able to eat almost anything. You can give them rich and exotic dishes – they adore them – but, as they get older, this love of the lush life can make them liverish.

Their birth salt is sulphate of soda and a deficiency of this can produce liver ailments and diabetes. Like Aries people they need celery which happens to be full of sodium as well as potassium. Apples, lettuce, radishes, strawberries and spinach all have a high content of sodium. One of the most vital functions of this salt is its effect on the digestive juices.

It is worth noting that Taurean women, while loving good cooking are apt not to take a lot of trouble in the kitchen themselves. So it is a bonus for them when they go out for a meal. The Taurean of both sexes is often a stylist, appreciating care taken to decorate a table or set off a dish and being more interested and critical than most as to what wine is served with which course.

Chicken and beef dishes with a "difference" are favoured by Taureans, especially chicken Kiev and beef Stroganoff. They also adore anything cooked in wine, but are apt to turn up their noses at plain cooking.

Swiss Rosti Potatoes

Enough for 2 or 3

Ingredients: 1 lb. of potatoes; 1½ oz. pure lard; 1 small chopped onion; chopped parsley; freshly ground black pepper.

Method: Peel potatoes and parboil in boiling, lightly salted water for about 8–9 minutes. Drain potatoes and then grate potatos and onions, seasoning with a little freshly ground black pepper. Heat lard in a frying pan until very hot; add potatoes and onion, using palette knife to prevent ingredients sticking to the sides of the pan, and also to form a small wall. Fry lightly for 6 or 7 minutes until golden brown; place plate over potatoes, reverse pan and slide unbrowned side of potatoes into pan. Cook until golden. Then slide on to dish with palette knife and serve very hot, garnishing with a little chopped parsley.

Russian Fish Pie

Enough for 3–4

Ingredients: 8 oz. short crust pastry; 10 oz. cod, or tinned pink salmon; 2 chopped hard-boiled eggs; 1 dessertspoon of chopped parsley; 2 oz. boiled rice (long grain); 1 small, chopped onion; 1 tablespoon mayonnaise; 1 oz. butter; 2 tablespoons milk; cayenne pepper and salt to taste.

Method: Roll out pastry into oblong, moistening edge with a little milk. Mix together thoroughly all the other ingredients, then spread the mixture on the pastry and roll up into a long roll, sealing the edges with pastry. Clip the top with scissors and brush with milk. Place in oven at 425 degrees (electric) and cook for 40 minutes, reducing heat after 20 minutes. Serve hot, though this dish can be eaten cold.

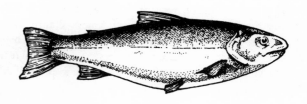

Chicken in Paprika

Enough for 2 or 3

Ingredients: 3 chicken breasts; 1 onion; ¼ lb. button mushrooms; 1 small red pepper; ½ teaspoon ground garlic; salt and pepper to taste; ¼ pint double cream; 2 oz. butter; 1½ tablespoons plain flour; 1 dessertspoon chopped parsley; 1 teaspoon paprika.

Method: Mix flour, salt and paprika, coating chicken pieces with this mixture. Heat 1 ounce of the butter and fry chicken gently until golden brown; cover, reduce heat and cook for 30 minutes. Peel and chop onion; wash and slice mushrooms. Cut top off red pepper and remove seeds; cut into thin strips. Lightly cook the pepper, mushrooms etc. in the remaining butter for 7 minutes, then add ground garlic and cream. Heat, but do not boil; finally place chicken on a hot dish, cover with sauce and sprinkle with chopped parsley.

Steamed Celery in Cheese Sauce

Enough for 2

Ingredients: 1 root of celery (wash well and cut into 5 inch-long pieces); 3 oz. Irish Cheddar cheese (grated); 1 oz. plain flour; 1 oz. butter; ½ pint milk; pepper.

Method: Steam celery in steamer until tender (about 15–20 minutes). Mix flour, pepper and butter together into a paste. Heat milk in saucepan and pour into paste, returning whole mixture to saucepan, stirring all the time on a lower heat until thick. Gently boil for 1 minute, then simmer gently for 2 minutes. Add all but ½ oz. of the grated cheese. Place celery in an oven-proof dish; pour the mixture over the celery and sprinkle the remaining cheese on top, grilling until golden brown.

Baked Apples Stuffed with Cherries and Chopped Almonds

Enough for 2 or 3 persons)

Ingredients: 3 tablespoons double cream; 2 oz. glacé cherries;
3 medium-sized cooking apples; 2 oz. split, blanched almonds;
1 tablespoon liquid honey; 1 tablespoon brown sugar; 1 oz. butter;
2 tablespoons water.

Method: Wash apples and remove cores, using a core-remover, cut
around to prevent breaking. Cut cherries into small pieces, mixing
with almonds. Stuff the apples with cherries and almonds, placing in an
oven-proof dish. Pour honey and sugar over the apples and put knobs
of butter on each apple. Cook in the oven in the two tablespoons of
water for ½–¾ hour; just before serving pour a tablespoon of cream over
each apple.

The Birthday Menu

Avocado pear with prawns

Beef Stroganoff

Pineapple Fritters

Coffee and Brandy or Calvados

Wine: Prince Noir (Barton and Guestier, red)

The Birthday Menu

The avocado pear with prawns should present no problem, if preparing at home. Simply select a ripe avocado, cut in two, remove the stone and fill each half with a few fresh or tinned prawns. Serve with a mayonnaise sauce. If you wish to make the mayonnaise yourself, use the yolk of one egg (if for 2 persons); a pinch of pepper and salt; 1 teaspoon of tarragon; ½ pint of salad oil; 1 dessertspoon of cream; 1 dessertspoon tarragon vinegar; Angostura bitters. Put the yolk in a saucepan, add salt and pepper, stir with a wooden spoon and add the salad oil a drop a time, then more quickly as you stir the mixture. Add in drops of tarragon vinegar alternatively with the salad oil, also the tarragon. Finally add the cream, stirring all the time. Work in the drops of Angostura bitters until the mixture has a slight (repeat slight) pinkish hue.

For the beef Stroganoff you will require (for 2 persons): 1 lb. Porterhouse steak (or fillet); 1 tablespoon butter; 1 medium-sized onion; ½ lb. button mushrooms; 1 tablespoon flour; 1 cup milk; 1 tablespoon heavy cream; a few sprigs of parsley; salt and freshly ground black pepper. Cut the beef into thin slivers about ½ inch thick and cook in butter until lightly browned. Add the onion and mushrooms. Brown the flour and add to the onion and mushrooms. Then add milk, cream and seasoning, simmering on a low heat and stirring the whole mixture until it is thick. Then pour the whole mixture into a large bowl and sprinkle with parsley. You can serve this with sauté potatoes and carrots.

Use either fresh pineapple or tinned pineapple (rings not cubes) for the fritters. Cut up the pineapple rings, coating them with batter, and then fry in hot fat until nicely browned. Drain well, sprinkle with castor sugar and serve.

Recipes For Gemini

21 May — 20 June

Geminians are sometimes difficult to cater for. It is a case of finding out what kind of a mood they are in. Many of them have a tendency to vacillate between hearty eating, thoroughly enjoying everything set before them, and cutting down on their food intake for a whole week or more.

On the other hand, if you manage to please a Geminian foodwise, he or she can be most appreciative. This particularly applies to the women.

They belong to what are known as the Air signs, which include those born under the signs of Libra and Aquarius as well. It is always dangerous to read too much into the alleged characteristics of the Air signs as a whole and always safer to stick to just one sign of the zodiac at a time, or at least to signs having similar birth salts. But, if you really want to be daring and experimental, or even to risk a snub or a laugh at your expense, bear in mind that those belonging to the Air signs are said to be "turned on" by what they like to believe is a sexy aphrodisiac diet. This especially applies to some Geminians.

However, if you have a sense of humour, you will refrain from telling them that their birth salt is potassium chloride and that lack of this can cause catarrh, swollen glands, sore throats, a sluggish liver and constipation.

It is notorious that those born under Gemini often tax their nervous systems by tackling too many things at once. This usually happens if they neglect to stock up their required amount of potassium chloride. Most of the foods which suit Aries-types can be taken by Geminians, who should also have plenty of vegetables such as turnips, green beans, cauliflower and Brussels sprouts. Salads which include a few ingredients such as sorrel, cottage cheese and spinach make an excellent choice.

One point to remember is that those born under this sign usually have a special fondness for strawberries. When nothing else seems to tempt them, they can often be lured into eating large quantities of strawberries – especially the female Gemini! But those of both sexes enjoy a sense ot style in the presentation of meals and the atmosphere of a dinner party is as important to them as the dinner itself. It is a gamble, of course, as no two Geminians are absolutely alike in all things, but give them oysters by candlelight and they will think that is a really sexy meal.

Veal with Mushrooms and White Wine

For 2 persons

Ingredients: 1 lb. of pie veal in whole piece; 4 medium-sized carrots; ½ lb. mushrooms; 1½ oz. butter; 1 oz. plain flour; 1 dessertspoon lemon juice; 3 tablespoons double cream; 1 level tablespoon chopped parsley; 4 quarters of lemon; 2 bayleaves; 1 medium-sized onion; 1 wine glass of medium dry white wine; 8–10 oz. noodles.

Method: Trim meat and cut into 1½ inch pieces. Blanch in boiling water for 3 minutes over heat. Drain and return meat to pan with onion and carrots cut into cubes; cover with wine and water, bring to the boil; cover pan and gently simmer for 1 hour. Add whole button mushrooms after they have been washed and dried and cook for a further 20 minutes. Mix flour and butter to smooth paste in medium basin; strain liquid into ½ pint measure. Keep meat hot and then pour the ½ pint liquid into butter and flour paste, stirring until smooth. Return to saucepan, bring to the boil, stirring all the time and cook for 4 minutes. Add lemon juice and meat mixture; then heat together. Just before serving add cream; turn on to hot serving dish, garnishing with chopped parsley and lemon quarters. Serve with boiled noodles, which after cooking have been mixed with a little butter.

Purée of Kale with Cream

Enough for 2

Ingredients: 1½ lbs. of kale; 4 tablespoons of cream; 1 oz. butter; pinch of nutmeg; pepper and salt.

Method: Remove stalk from kale, wash thoroughly. Place in sufficient salt water to cover which should be brought to the boil first; cover saucepan and cook for 10–15 minutes. Strain well, then chop kale finely; replace in saucepan, adding butter, and heat. When hot add cream, nutmeg and seasoning; place on hot dish and serve.

Porterhouse Steak with Olives and Anchovies

Enough for 2

Ingredients: 2 knobs of butter mixed with teaspoon of lemon juice; 2 1½ inch thick porterhouse steaks; 1 small tin of anchovies; 5 oz. green olives, not stuffed; a little olive oil or melted butter; black pepper and salt to taste.

Method: Trim steaks and wipe with damp cloth. Brush with olive oil or melted butter on both sides. Place steaks under pre-heated grill, grilling on both sides for 5–8 minutes. Place on hot dish and arrange anchovies on the steaks to form a criss-cross pattern. Then place the olives around the steaks. Put in a hot oven for 5 minutes and just before serving put knobs of firm butter on steaks.

Fresh Pineapple and Strawberry Salad with Kirsch

Ingredients: ½ a fresh pineapple; ½ lb. fresh strawberries;
1 tablespoon lemon juice; 2 tablespoons clear Acacia honey;
1 tablespoon Kirsch liqueur.

Method: Peel pineapple and remove eyes; wash strawberries and remove stalks; then place in glass bowl with pineapple. Mix lemon juice and honey together and then add Kirsch and poor over fruit. Place in refrigerator for ½ hour before serving.

Mushroom and Celery Soup

Enough for 2–3 persons

Ingredients: ½ lb. button mushrooms; 1½ tablespoons butter;
1½ pints stock (soup made from carcass of chicken or chicken stock cube); 3 sticks of celery; 1 medium-sized potato; 1 level tablespoon of chopped chives or the green of spring onions; freshly ground black pepper and salt to taste; small knob of butter.

Method: Wash and drain mushrooms (do not peel); cut into slices and fry lightly in pan with celery: do not brown. Put stock into saucepan and bring to boil. Peel and slice potato and add to boiling stock, then simmer for 10–15 minutes until tender. Add the mushrooms and celery and cook for further 7 minutes. Season with salt and pepper; place in soup bowls or tureen; sprinkle with chopped chives or green of onions, adding small knob of butter. Then serve, garnished with croutons fried in butter, if you wish.

The Birthday Menu

Oysters
(Colchesters or Whitstables, if in UK, Blue Points if in
the USA, but try to avoid having Portuguese)

Mushroom omelette with
mixed salad

Strawberries and Cream
(an added bonus, if you can add a large glass of
cointreau to the strawberries)

Wine: Champagne
(If you can afford it, and bear in mind that Moet
Chandon offer probably the best non-vintage champagne.)
Alternatively, go for a Chablis.

Coffee and Cointreau or Armagnac brandy

The Birthday Menu

This is a relatively simple meal to try out at home, if you wish. Do not on any account buy oysters that are already opened. Open them yourself with a sharp kitchen knife and serve with fresh lemon juice and red pepper. For the omelettes you simply require: 4 eggs (for 2 persons), 3 oz. button mushrooms; 2 dessertspoons of cream or milk (optional); salt and pepper. Frankly, you will get the best results with a plain egg and mushroom omelette, omitting milk or cream, but that is a matter of taste. Fry the mushrooms lightly in butter until slightly brown; then remove and chop into small pieces, but not too small. Have a frying pan with cooking oil or butter at maximum heat and then, when you have whipped up the eggs long enough to marry yolks and whites, pour half the mixture into the pan, leaving the remainder for the second omelette. The pieces of mushroom should be sprinkled on to the mixture once it has slightly firmed up. Then, when a little firmer, fold over to make a half-moon shaped omelette. Turn when golden brown and repeat for the second omelette. Serve with a mixed salad of tomatoes, lettuce, celery, cucumber, chicory and black olives.

Strawberries and cream are enhanced if the strawberries are soaked in a little cointreau, taking care to remove the stalks first and to choose only firm, and not over-ripe strawberries.

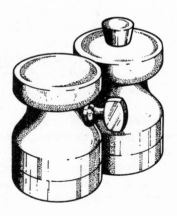

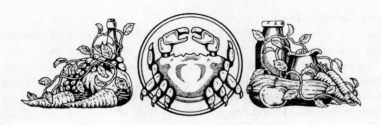

Recipes For Cancer

21 June — 20 July

An astrologically-minded friend of mine once said rather flippantly: "You have a Cancer-type coming in tonight – that's quite simple. You just give him a crab sandwich!"

The sign of Cancer is, of course, the Crab and it would seem logical to think that Cancerians like this shellfish.

The truth is, however, slightly different. It might well be that your Cancer guest will love crab sandwiches, or dressed crab and salad. Like those born under Scorpio and Pisces, the Cancerian often has cravings for fish of all kinds. But he (or she) also tends to be allergic to some fish. They may not realise the allergy, as quite often it is masked. You, the host or hostess, have to find out what the allergy is. Alas, if you are not careful, you may only find out through a disastrous meal. But it is best to serve up the "safe" fish such as sole, plaice, turbot, even cod and not to chance oysters, shellfish or mackerel.

The sign of Cancer governs the stomach and the great need for Cancerians is to eat things which are well cooked and not to hurry their food. They are prone to stomach and liver ailments. Their birth salt is calcium fluoride, which is one of the major properties of the finger-nails, teeth, bones and muscular tissue. When calcium fluoride is deficient in the body of a Cancerian, lassitude and lack of energy occurs. By far the best way to make up this deficiency is by giving natural foods which are rich in calcium, especially milk, prunes, cottage cheese – a

36

valuable high protein content and calcium food – cabbage (both green and red), onions, raisins, parsley, watercress and among fruits, oranges and lemons.

One should avoid convenience foods for Cancerians, even though on their own they are notorious for relying on a tin opener. The fresher the foods the better the Cancerian's health. Many of them have a preference for Italian cooking.

Sardines on Toast Special

Enough for 2 persons
Ingredients: 1 tin of large sardines in oil; 1 small onion; 1 small tomato; black ground pepper and salt to taste; juice of ½ lemon; 1 oz. grated Cheddar cheese; 1½ oz. butter; 2 pieces of toast; 6 stuffed olives.

Method: Butter toast and place slices of tomato on top of each piece, sprinkling with salt. Then lay the sardines, without the oil, on the tomatoes. Cover sardines with the onion slices; season with pepper, add grated cheese and put under low grill, cooking until brown. Serve with fresh green salad.

Cottage Cheese Salad

Enough for 2 persons
Ingredients: 1 large box of cottage cheese; 1 dessertspoon chopped parsley; a few sprigs of watercress; 1 heart of lettuce; 2 tablespoons sunflower seed oil; a few pieces of pineapple (fresh or cubes); 2 chopped spring onions; black pepper and salt; 1 tablespoon of mayonnaise, either home made or Benedictine Mayonnaise.

Method: Thoroughly wash lettuce, watercress, onions and parsley and drain well. Mix oil, lemon juice, salt and pepper together until mixture is thick. Chop pineapple roughly and mix with cottage cheese, adding chopped onion. Place lettuce on dish and then put the cottage cheese mixture in the centre. Sprinkle oil mixture over lettuce leaves. Top cottage cheese with mayonnaise and chopped parsley and put sprigs of watercress around the base.

Lamb Chops in Piquant Sauce

Enough for 2 or 3 persons

Ingredients: 3 lamb chops (good chump chops are best); 6 stuffed olives chopped; a little oil; 2 tablespoons tomato chutney; 1½ tablespoons red currant jelly; 1–2 teaspoons soya sauce; 1 dessertspoon chopped onion; 1 dessertspoon chopped parsley.

Method: Wipe chops with damp cloth, then brush over with oil. Place in frying pan and fry for 10–15 minutes, turning once when brown. Place on serving dish and keep hot. Add to the pan chopped onion and gently fry for a few minutes; add other ingredients and, when thoroughly hot, spoon over chops, finally sprinkling the whole with chopped parsley. Then serve.

Courgettes in Savoury Sauce

Enough for 2

Ingredients: ¾ lb. courgettes (baby marrows); 3 medium tomatoes; 1 oz. butter; ½ teaspoon ground garlic; a little sugar, salt and pepper to taste; ½ teaspoon grated nutmeg.

Method: Wipe courgettes with damp cloth; remove stalk and cut off tip of other end and then cut into 1 inch slices. Cook in a little boiling, salted water for 5–10 minutes until just tender. Peel tomatoes (easily done if placed in boiling water for a minute); slice and add tomatoes to butter melted in saucepan on low heat. Bring slowly to the boil, lower heat and cook for about 10 minutes until you have a thick sauce; add garlic, pepper, salt, sugar and grated nutmeg. Drain courgettes well and add to sauce, mixing carefully. Place on hot serving dish.

Purée of Chestnut Flan

Enough for 3-4

Ingredients: 1 sponge flan case; 1 tin of sweet chestnut purée; 1 wine glass of sherry or Madeira; 5 oz. whipped cream; 5 glacé cherries; a little angelica; 1 oz. toasted split almonds.

Method: Soak base of flan case in half the sherry (or Madeira). Place the purée of chestnut in basin with remains of sherry and mix thoroughly. Then place in flan case, spreading whipped cream over chestnut purée and fluff up with fork. Make stalks with angelica and stick in cherries; then place cherries on top of cream and sprinkle with toasted split almonds. Put in refrigerator for $\frac{1}{2}$ hour and then serve.

The Birthday Menu

Turtle Soup with sherry

Grilled Dover Sole with
Peas & Mushrooms

Fresh Fruit Salad and Cream

Coffee with Strega liqueur

Wine: One of the Niersteiner Hocks,
or a Blue Nun

The Birthday Menu

This is another birthday meal which can perhaps be conjured up as well at home as at a restaurant. The turtle soup may pose some problems unless you are prepared to use a tin of such soup. By adding a tablespoon of a medium sherry to such a soup, you could make the first course easy enough. Otherwise it would be a question of obtaining a quarter of a pound of sun-dried turtle which would need to be soaked for 3 whole days beforehand, changing the water twice daily, and then adding various other items. But these other items can just as easily be added to the tinned turtle soup with equally good effects; they are a bouquet-garni of bay-leaf, thyme, basil and marjoram; a dessertspoon of lemon-juice; 1 clove; tiny slices of carrot. Choose your Dover Sole carefully, ensuring that it is fresh and firm. Trim it and wipe with a damp cloth, smear it with heated butter and sprinkle with salt and pepper. Then grill by gas or electricity in a greased fire-proof dish for about 4 minutes to each side. Serve garnished with slices of lemon and sprigs of parsley, with peas and grilled mushrooms, perferably the button variety. The fresh fruit salad can ideally be made with thin slices of banana, apple, orange, pear and pineapple and some halved white grapes. Finely chopped almonds can be added, if you wish. Add a dessertspoon of Benedictine.

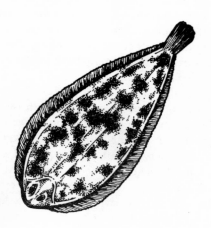

Recipes For Leo

21 July — 21 August

Two points to bear in mind about Leonians is that the men, if not the women, tend to be hearty eaters with appetites that last through every course of a meal. Often, too, they enjoy a drink rather more than most; a Leonian would probably prefer you to set down a large carafe of a cheap wine before him than a half bottle of one of better quality. On the other hand Leonians can be discriminating, too.

Some of them tend to be gourmets in rather a flamboyant manner, enjoying showing off as people with special tastes as much as anything else. But never forget that those born under the sign of Leo often come back for another helping. The female Leonian is very often not domesticated and does not herself like cooking. But they enjoy eating out in grandiose surroudings, though many will be happy to indulge in an al fresco meal, or a barbecue or picnic.

Though they have great vitality, those born under this sign of the zodiac need to watch putting too much strain on the heart as they grow older. This certainly applies to their diet where they are so apt to over-indulge themselves. Their birth salt is magnesium phosphate which helps to build nerve tissue, to keep blood pressure at normal and to give the muscles flexibility. While this salt can be taken in tablet form, like many other of the birth salts there are a number of foods which are rich in magnesium phosphate. Among vegetables, cabbage, peas, sugar beet and lettuce are to be recommended and plums have a high content of both phosphate and magnesium.

Leonians usually prefer substantial meals to gourmet dishes, though there are a few exceptions to this as has been indicated and, if you can find out the Leonian's special delight in this direction, you will be rewarded by the enthusiasm with which he or she receives it. But on the whole they like such dishes as Spaghetti Bolognaise rather than Lobster in Aspic and a massive Paella rather than a Sole Veronique. They also have a fondness for a mixture of sweet and sour in both occidental and oriental dishes, and most of them would prefer a sweet course to biscuits and cheese; some Leonians (admittedly a minority, but not such a small one) actually dislike cheese.

Savoury Ginger Mince
Enough for 2 persons
Ingredients: ½ lb. minced beef, or from left-over roast beef; 6 shallots; ½ teaspoon grated nutmeg; 4 pieces of chopped stem ginger, or crystalised ginger; 1 oz. butter; 2 tablespoons of tomato purée; salt and pepper to taste; boiled rice.

Method: Peel and chop shallots; place butter in saucepan over low heat, add shallots and gently cook for 6 minutes. Add minced beef to shallots and cook for a further 6 minutes. Add ginger and tomato purée, and cook for a further 7 minutes, seasoning to taste with salt and pepper. Then place on a serving dish with a border of boiled rice. Serve with a green salad mixed with oil and vinegar.

Casserole of Pork Chops

Enough for 2 persons

Ingredients: 2 pork chops; 1 level tablespoon of plain flour; 2 tablespoons sunflower seed oil; 8 shallots, peeled and left whole, or small onions; 1 small red pepper, sliced with seed and stalk removed; 4 oz. button mushrooms (washed); 8 dried apricots soaked overnight; a little soya sauce; 1 tablespoon of tomato purée; ½ pint chicken stock or chicken stock cube; casserole.

Method: Heat the oil in frying pan, then gently fry the shallots in it until they are lightly browned; then place them on a plate. Dip the chops in seasoned flour and then lightly cook in the oil until brown. Mix the remaining flour with fat in pan and add chicken stock, shallots, red pepper, cut into thin slices, the liquid from the soaked apricots, soya sauce and tomato purée: bring to the boil, stirring all the time. Then place the chops in the casserole; pour the sauce over them and cook in a moderate oven for 1½ hours. Ten minutes before the end of cooking add the apricots.

Peas and Spring Onions

Enough for 2 persons

Ingredients: 1½ lb. fresh garden peas, shelled; 1 small bunch of spring onions; 1 oz. butter; 1 teaspoon of flour; pepper and salt to taste.

Method: Having shelled peas and cleaned spring onions, bring a little water to the boil. Add peas and spring onions to boiling water, cover saucepan and cook for 7–10 minutes on a gentle heat. Then place peas and onions in vegetable dish. Mix butter and flour in basin, adding seasoning; then pour water in which peas and onions boiled into the butter mixture. Return to the saucepan and cook gently for 5 minutes until mixture is smooth, stirring all the time. Then pour over the peas and serve.

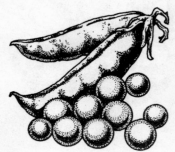

Noodle Pie with Minced Chicken and Mushrooms
Enough for 3
Ingredients: 1 tablespoon sunflower seed oil; 4 oz. left-over chicken (minced); 2 oz. button mushrooms; 8 oz. noodles (Quick Tagliatelle suggested); a little coarse ground garlic or 1 clove of crushed garlic (optional); 1 small onion; salt and ground black pepper to taste; 1 level dessertspoon cornflour; 1½ oz. butter; 1½ oz. grated Gruyère cheese; ½ teaspoon grated nutmeg; ½ to ¾ pint of chicken stock; 2 tablespoons of cream.

Method: Mince chicken; wipe mushrooms with damp cloth and cut into slices, adding garlic. Chop up onion coarsely; heat oil in saucepan and add onion, cooking gently for 5 minutes. Do not brown. Add chicken, mushrooms, seasoning, nutmeg and cook gently for 7 minutes. Mix cornflour with a little of stock, adding to chicken mixture. Then pour in remainder of stock and gently bring to the boil, cooking for 2–3 minutes. Cook the noodles for 3–4 minutes, drain well; then mix with chicken ingredients, placing in ovenproof dish. Sprinkle with the grated cheese and butter cut into small pieces. Cook under grill until nicely browned.

Mixed Fruit Trifle
Enough for 2–3 persons
Ingredients: ¾ pint fresh orange juice; 3 crumbled sponge cakes; 1 level dessertspoon powdered gelatine; 1 peeled orange and the peeled segments of the orange; 1 medium-sized pear; 1 medium-sized apple; 1 medium-sized peach; ½ lb. cherries (stoned); 1 tablespoon Benedictine liqueur (optional); juice of half a lemon; ½ pint double cream; 1 tablespoon honey; 6 unstoned cherries with stalks for decoration.

Method: Cut the pear, apple and peach into small pieces. Dissolve the gelatine in a little water in a pint basin over hot water until transparent; add orange and lemon juice and honey to gelatine; allow almost to set. Crumble the sponge cakes into a glass dish or bowl; add the fruit, mix together (except unstoned cherries kept for decoration.) Pour over this the nearly set jelly, place in the refrigerator and allow to set firm. Whip cream, add Benedictine (optional), cover the top of the trifle with the cream, fork into points and decorate with the cherries.

The Birthday Menu

Ravioli or Ratatouille

Noisettes of lamb Henri IV
(cooked with sherry and served on croutes with
spinach and bearnaise sauce)
with new potatoes and peas

Melon soaked in
crême de menthe

Coffee and Courvoisier brandy

Wine: A light claret or
a red chianti

The Birthday Menu

Two choices are suggested for the first course for the Leonian meal, chiefly because, if you decide to cook it at home, time may well be a vital factor. To make ravioli yourself is not only a highly skilled process, but takes up a great deal of time. So you may wish to settle for the tinned ravioli which only needs warming up and serving sprinkled with Parmesan cheese. But, if you don't want Leo to suspect the use of tinned food, then try the ratatouille. For 2 persons you will require: 1 medium-sized onion; 1 small aubergine; 1 small green pepper; a small clove of garlic; 2 tomatoes, peeled; 1 dessertspoon chopped parsley; 3 tablespoons olive oil; 1 courgette; salt and ground black pepper to taste; a small pinch of tarragon; a small pinch of lemon thyme; a dash of nutmeg. Having skinned and sliced the onion, washed the pepper and aubergine, you cut the pepper in quarters and remove the seeds from the former and the stalk from the aubergine. Heat the oil in a frying pan until very hot, put in the sliced onion and cook for 5 minutes, but do not allow to brown. Then add the pepper and aubergine and cook for another 3 minutes. Meanwhile cut the tops from the courgette and cut into slices. Slice the tomatoes and then put tomatoes and courgette into the frying pan. Reduce the heat, cover the pan with a lid and leave to simmer for 30–40 minutes. Then add the garlic, seasoning and herbs and simmer for another 5 minutes. Serve hot from the pan.

Some restaurants specialise in the Noisettes of Lamb Henri IV, which, at its best, is a splendid dish. You can turn out something less pretentious, though quite as good, at home. You will require: a fillet of lamb cut into 4 pieces; 3 oz. butter; 4 croutes of white bread fried in butter; salt and ground black pepper to taste; ½ pint of Béchamel sauce; 6 oz. button mushrooms; ½ oz. of chopped parsley. Wipe the mushrooms with a damp cloth, remove the stalks and then cook them in 1 oz. of butter for 5 minutes, but do not brown. Put aside and finely chop the stalks. Make the Béchamel sauce in the usual way – 1 oz. butter, ¾ oz. plain flour, melting the butter and adding the flour, cooking gently for 2 minutes, stirring continuously. Add some heated milk and cook for 4 minutes, stirring all the time. Add the chopped mushroom stalks. Fry the croutes of bread, place on a hot dish and keep warm. Cook the fillets of lamb in the remainder of butter for 4 minutes on each side until well browned. Place the fillets on the croutes; then put the mushrooms on the fillets and spoon on to each fillet the mushroom sauce. Sprinkle with parsley and serve immediately. You can

47

add a little sherry to the sauce, if you wish. But the dish is quite splendid as it is and can be served with new potatoes and peas, or croquette potatoes and spinach.

For the dessert you make boats out of large slices of melon, removing the seeds and carving out the fruit of the melon. A very ripe melon is required. Chop up the fruit of the melon together with some sweet white grapes and minute slivers of apple. Fill the melon boats with this and pour crême de menthe over each in liberal portions. Decorate with green glacé cherries.

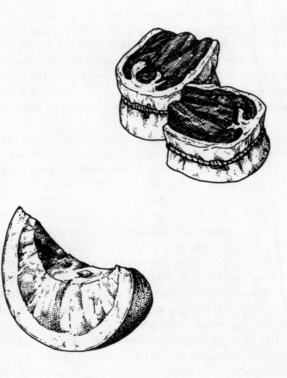

Recipes For Virgo

22 August — 22 September

If you are a Virgoan yourself, take heed because your love of rich foods may cause you to put on weight. On the other hand, if you are entertaining Virgoans, bear in mind that one way to their hearts is to give them luxury foods. They adore caviare and truffles, French pastries filled with cream and *paella valenciana*. You can't get away with mundane dishes where they are concerned.

Their biochemical salt is potassium sulphate and a lack of this constituent can lead to a clogging of the pores, thus hindering the draining off of impurities from the system. On the whole Virgoans are healthy enough, but they need to watch their diet otherwise they are liable to stomach troubles and colds.

Salads containing potassium are especially good for Virgoans – grated carrots, shredded cabbage leaves, cucumber, lettuce with lemon juice. Tomato, onion and celery soups are also recommended. Some Virgoans can be enraptured by fish soups, or even fish stews. Most of them love game and especially the smaller birds such as quail and pigeon.

Yet the Virgoan is also a complex and somewhat enigmatic and contradictory character – not unlike the Virgin Queen, Elizabeth I, who made a virtue of being all things to all people. A Virgoan is often disgustingly healthy, yet can be a great worrier over his or her health, apt to imagine things are wrong with them when they are not. This turns them from a love of rich foods to a sudden fad for health foods and dishes of all kinds. But even the latter will tend to be exotic, or at least comprised of exotic and little-known or used herbs. Virgoans of this type keep their kitchen cupboards filled with all manner of herbs and spices and sometimes vegetarian substitutes for meat.

It is as well to find out beforehand if your Virgoan guest is in a food-fad mood. What you can be sure of is that all of them like pronounced seasoning in their foods, preferably with herbs, but often with strong, tangy spices. They love thyme, cinnamon, rosemary, poke-root, tarragon, tumeric and valerian.

Prawn Salad with Smoked Salmon and Mussels

As hors d'oeuvre for 2 persons

Ingredients: ½ pint fresh mussels (optional and make sure first that your guest is not one of the very few Virgoans who either avoid or dislike mussels); 1 pint of prawns in shells; 2 oz. smoked salmon; 1 tablespoon of chopped chives; ground black pepper to taste; 1 teaspoon cider vinegar; 2 tablespoons mayonnaise; 1 dessertspoon dry white wine (an *ordinaire* will do); 1 small onion.

Method: Shell prawns, place in small salad or hors d'oeuvres dish. Slice smoked salmon in very thin strips. Wash through the mussels in salt water; put in saucepan with small quantity of water and small onion; then cover and cook for 5–8 minutes, until shells are open. Remove mussels from shells and allow to cool; then mix together with the prawns and smoked salmon. Make a mixture of white wine, cider vinegar and mayonnaise, stirring well before adding the mixture of prawns, salmon and mussels. Sprinkle with chopped chives before serving.

Pigeon in Cream and Herbs

Enough for 2–3 persons for main dish

Ingredients: 2 pigeons (young), plucked and dressed; 2 oz.
butter; 2 tablespoons olive oil; 1 small carton of double cream;
ground black pepper and salt to taste; 1 teaspoon chopped parsley;
1 teaspoon chopped oregano; 1 teaspoon chopped chives;
1 teaspoon chopped spring onions; 1 level tablespoon cornflour;
2 tablespoons brandy; ½ pint of stock; 4 triangles of white bread
from which to make fried bread.

Method: Cut pigeons in half length-wise. Melt butter in heavy pan,
lightly browning the pigeons on a gentle heat for 10 minutes. Place
pigeons in casserole, season with pepper and salt and add stock; cover
the casserole and put in a moderate oven for 30–40 minutes. Mix cornflour with cream and then mix with stock from pigeons. Pour this
mixture over the pigeons, add herbs and cook for another 10–15 minutes. Fry triangles of bread in olive oil and just before serving put
fried bread on top of the pigeons in the casserole and serve piping hot.

Mushrooms Greek Style

Ingredients: ½ lb. button mushrooms; 1 small onion cut in rings;
1 wine glass dry white wine; juice of half a lemon; ground black
pepper and salt to taste; half teaspoon brown sugar; 1 level
teaspoon coriander seeds; 1 teaspoon chopped parsley; 1 bouquet
garni of thyme, rosemary, oregano, bayleaf and marjoram (this can
be obtained from any good delicatessen shop); 4 tablespoons olive
oil, 1 teaspoon tomato purée.

Method: Wipe mushrooms with damp cloth. Place oil, wine, lemon
juice, bouquet garni, seasoning, onion, brown sugar, coriander seeds
in saucepan; heat and then add mushrooms and tomato purée. Cook in
covered pan for 5–7 minutes. Then place in bowl and leave in refrigerator overnight. Serve very cold and sprinkle with chopped parsley.

Cucumber Soup

Enough for 3 persons

Ingredients: 1 large cucumber; ½ lb. potatoes; 1¼ pints water; 4 tablespoons of cream (single); pepper and salt to taste; 1 level tablespoon plain flour; 1 oz. butter; 1 small onion finely chopped; 1 dessertspoon of finely chopped tarragon.

Method: Peel potatoes and cut into small pieces. Peel cucumber, remove seeds and cut into small pieces. Bring water to boil; add cucumber, potatoes, onion and cook gently for 1 hour to 75 minutes. Then sieve soup. Carefully mix flour and butter to a smooth paste in bowl and add soup. Return to the saucepan and slowly bring to the boil. Cook for 2 minutes, then pour into soup tureen and add cream, serving immediately.

Purée of Chestnuts with Chocolate and Cream

Enough for 2–3 persons

Ingredients: 1 large tin of sweet chestnut purée; 1 slab of plain cooking chocolate; 3 tablespoons Tia Maria liqueur; 2 oz. chopped, toasted, blanched almonds; 8 Maraschino cherries; 5 oz. of double cream.

Method: Place the purée of chestnut in a basin. Break the chocolate into small pieces; place in a saucepan with half the Tia Maria and stir until completely melted. Mix half the chocolate with the purée of chestnut and add the remainder of the Tia Maria. Rinse a basin in cold water (to prevent sticking); put alternatively in the basin a layer of purée of chestnut and a layer of the melted chocolate. Allow to set in the refrigerator and, when set, turn out on to a large plate. Decorate around the base and on top with the whipped cream. Place a cherry on top in the centre and the remainder of the cherries around the base.

The Birthday Menu

Pâté de foie gras aux truffes

Paella Valenciana

Millefeuille

Wine: Anjou Rosé

Coffee and Kummel liqueur

The Birthday Menu

If you plan to try out this meal at home, you can at least limit your problems in that the *pâté de foie gras aux truffes* and the millefeuille can be bought in most high class stores. This will enable you to concentrate your efforts entirely on the *paella Valenciana*. This is a dish on which it pays to lavish much care and attention. For a meal for two you require: ½ oz. butter; 5 oz. Patna rice; 1 dessertspoon oil; 3 or 4 strands of saffron; ½ large onion; 4 oz. diced chicken; 2 tomatoes; ½ green pepper; 1 crushed clove of garlic; 2 oz. prawns; a small pot of mussels; parsley; 2 oz. cockles.

First of all, melt the butter with the oil in a large pan. Fry the onion, green pepper and garlic, then season. Add the rice, a few spoonfuls at a time, to this mixture, stirring all the time, for about 2 minutes over a high temperature. Soak the saffron strands in half a pint of boiling water for 5 minutes. Then strain the liquid into the pan and stir vigorously, eventually bringing to the boil. Chop the tomatoes into slices and put these, together with the diced chicken, cockles and some of the prawns, into the pan, stirring all the time and mixing so that the ingredients are spread evenly. Cook for about 20 minutes – ideally in a casserole dish in the oven, but you can do it in the pan, except that you must then keep stirring and take care that the rice becomes fluffy and not overdone. Finally, add the mussels and the rest of the prawns and sprinkle on chopped parsley.

Recipes For Libra

23 September — 22 October

Librans are apt to be strongly romantic types and very easily depressed by drab surroundings or an uncongenial atmosphere. It is no use taking a Libran for lunch in a small, crowded café where food and drinks have been slopped over a filthy plastic table.

Kidney trouble is something to which Librans are very prone: to guard against this they should drink lots of cold water. However, apart from this and a slight tendency towards diabetes in later life, they are healthy people who enjoy good living. Invariably they have a very sweet tooth and this is something which you can pander to within reason. They have a passion for colourful, exotic sweets – trifles full of sherry or marsala and cream, pancakes filled with honey and liqueur. Nonetheless they are advised against too rich a diet, partly because of the kidney trouble. So if you entertain a Libran, if you lash out on a really sensational sweet, go easy on the main course and vice versa.

Sodium phosphate is their vital salt which helps to keep an equilibrium between the ordinary fluids of the body and the acids. Librans' diet should in this respect be similar in some respects to that of Taureans. Indeed, Librans and Taureans are easy to cater for at one and the same time.

It is the atmosphere which counts most when a Libran is lunching or dining out. Take him or her to a favourite restaurant, or, better still, to a new one that has some distinctive and original decor, and you will have scored before you take up the menu. If you are entertaining at home, you may find that some little touch in table decorations will make all the difference – a rose laid across her plate, or a pattern of petals around the table-cloth.

In food the Libran has catholic tastes ranging from the very simple to the *grande cuisine*. If you can sandwich one simple dish with something rather special, you will please the average Libran. And remember, although they appreciate table decorations, they abhor fussiness. One bowl of flowers too many and the Libran can be put off. It has been said that Librans like to look on food as a kind of aphrodisiac and that they are more interested in sex than food. I hope I haven't made the Libran sound too difficult. In fact, those of both sexes can be delightful guests and great fun. But it pays to find out beforehand all their little quirks which, by and large, are similar to those outlined above. Those Librans who are born close to the cusp of Virgo are apt to have marked allergies which vary from a refusal to eat tomatoes to an aversion to all shell-fish.

Roast Pheasant with Pâté and Grapes

Enough for 3–4 persons
Ingredients: 1 pheasant (cock pheasant is best), trussed and cleaned; 6 oz. liver pâté; 8 black grapes; 2 oz. butter; 2 rashers of streaky bacon; black ground pepper and salt to taste.

Method: Wipe pheasant with damp cloth; then gently rub all over with butter and seasoning, putting bacon rashers on the breast, then tie on with cotton to hold in place. Place pheasant in baking-tin and put in slow oven, about 300° and cook for about 1½ hours. For the last half hour remove bacon and turn up to 375°, browning pheasant all over. Then, 5 minutes before serving, spread liver paté over pheasant's breast; put grapes in baking-tin, leaving in oven for a further 5 minutes. Serve on hot dish, surrounded with the grapes and juices from the pheasant. Suggested accompaniments for serving: potato crisps (warmed) and green peas.

Baked Alaska

Enough for 3–4 persons

Ingredients: 1 sponge flan case or flat piece of sponge about the same size as the bottom of an ice-cream block; 1 ice-cream block, vanilla, raspberry ripple or other flavour; 1 punnet of raspberries, or other fresh fruit in season; 3 egg whites; 3 oz. granulated sugar; 4 tablespoons of cointreau, Benedictine or other liqueur; a few raspberries and split almonds.

Method: Clean raspberries or other fruits. Pour half the cointreau on the sponge cake and place on a dish. To make the meringue, separate egg whites from yolks into a large basin; whisk until stiff and standing in peaks. Add half the sugar and whisk until the meringue is stiff, smooth and shiny white; gently fold in the remainder of the sugar. Put half the ice-cream on the sponge cake and all but a few of the raspberries, which you leave for decorating. Pour the remainder of the cointreau over the raspberries, cover with the rest of the ice-cream; then quickly and completely cover the ice-cream with the meringue mixture, being very careful to go to the very base of the sponge. Slightly fork the meringue into peaks; decorate with raspberries and split almonds. Place in a very hot oven at 450° for 4–5 minutes until golden brown; remove from oven and serve immediately.

Potato and Tomato Soup

Enough for 3

Ingredients: 1 lb. ripe tomatoes; ¾ lb. potatoes; 1 medium-sized onion; 2 pints water; 2 oz. butter; pepper and salt to taste; small pieces of thin sliced bread for making croutons.

Method: Peel the potatoes, cut into small pieces; cut tomatoes into small pieces; chop up onion finely and then place all the ingredients into a good-sized saucepan. Add water and seasoning. Bring to the boil and allow to simmer for ¾ hour. Remove from the heat and pass through a sieve: return to saucepan. Heat and add butter; after which pour into soup tureen. Meanwhile fry the tiny pieces of bread in butter and oil to make croutons and serve these separately.

Chicory in Cheese

Enough for 2 persons

Ingredients: 4 medium-sized chicory; 2½ oz. grated cheese (Cheddar or Gruyère); 1 tablespoon white breadcrumbs; 2 oz. melted butter.

Method: Remove thin slice of stem from chicory; place in a little boiling water, then lower the heat and allow to simmer for 5–7 minutes. Drain well, as they are inclined to retain water. Place in oven-proof dish, covering the chicory with grated cheese and breadcrumbs. Then put in moderate oven for 15–20 minutes until lightly browned. Just before serving melt butter and pour over the ingredients.

Egg Plant and Tomatoes

Enough for 2–3 persons

Ingredients: 2 medium-sized aubergines; 6 medium-sized tomatoes; 2 oz. butter; 1 medium-sized chopped onion; ground black pepper and salt to taste; 1½ oz. grated Gruyère cheese (optional); 6 tablespoons of olive or sunflower seed oil.

Method: Put tomatoes into boiling water; remove and peel after having left them in the water for 1 minute. Cut tomatoes into pieces. Melt half the butter into a saucepan; add chopped onion and cook gently for 5 minutes; then add tomatoes and cook for 15–20 minutes until the whole is reduced to a thick sauce. Stir from time to time. Peel the aubergines and cut into half inch slices; then fry in hot oil until lightly browned. When cooked, place in an oven-proof dish a layer of aubergine and a layer of tomato mixture, finishing with a layer of tomato on top. If desired, cover with grated cheese. Top up with knobs of remaining butter and put into oven, cooking for ½ hour until a deep golden brown.

The Birthday Menu

Whitebait

Veal Normande
(a cutlet of veal with apple garnish and a
calvados sauce)

Pancakes filled with ice-cream
and served with almonds in a Tia Maria sauce
(alternatively Crêpes Suzette)

Coffee and a Parfait Amour liqueur
(or a cherry brandy)

Wine: Ideally, Le Pontet-Canet Bordeaux,
or some other white Bordeaux vintage

The Birthday Menu

Remember that Librans like being taken out, or entertained in restaurants, rather more than most people. They also like perfection. Add to this the fact that this menu is not exactly an easy one and you may decide to make this a night out rather than in. However, if you are determined, despite these warnings, to have a go, here is a plan of campaign. Leave your first course, the whitebait, until the very last thing just before the meal is due to commence. Sprinkle the whitebait with flour, carefully shaking off any excess flour that may get on in the process. Then cook the fish in a wire basket, which should be plunged into a deep pan of very hot oil or fat, keeping at a high heat for about 4–5 minutes. Keep moving the basket, swinging it around all the time and, when you remove it from the heat, shake well to get rid of the oil. The whitebait should then be put on kitchen paper or a cloth and left until all fat is strained off. Then serve on a very hot dish with slices of lemon and slices of thin, brown bread and butter, minus the crusts. The latter is a detail which Librans will appreciate.

For Veal Normande you will need for 2 persons: ¾ lb. of fillet or neck of veal; corn oil; ¼ teaspoon chopped parsley; a very little finely chopped lemon-rind; ½ lb. apples; 2 tablespoons Calvados; salt and pepper; 1 egg; breadcrumbs. Cut off thin slices of veal, trimming into cutlets. Whisk the egg and work in with it the parsley, lemon-rind, salt and pepper. Coat the cutlets with this mixture, add the breadcrumbs on top and fry until a golden brown. Peel the apples into thin slices, removing core, dip them in calvados and add into the pan, lightly frying. Drain off and place the slices of apple round a hot dish containing the cutlets. Then make a sauce of the juice remaining in the pan, plus some flour and the rest of the calvados, together with a few slivers of apple. Serve the sauce with the cutlets.

Serve with green beans and sweet corn.

You make your pancakes in the normal way, using enough for more than 2 persons, as with ice-cream being used, you don't want to be asked for a second helping. You should, therefore, offer a large portion first time. You require: ½ pint of milk; 3 oz. flour; 1 egg; pinch of salt; 2 oz. sultanas; split almonds, peeled; 2 oz. demerara sugar; 2 ozs. butter; 2 tablespoons Tia Maria liqueur; a vanilla or raspberry ice-cream block. Put the flour with a pinch of salt in a bowl, make a round space in the middle of the flour in the bowl and into this drop the egg, adding a little milk. Bring down the flour from the sides towards the centre and make a batter, beating the mixture until smooth, and then adding the remainder of the milk. When absolutely consistent pour the batter into a jug. Heat some oil in a pan and cook each pancake in turn by pouring the mixture from the jug into the hot pan. Wait until golden colour underneath and then turn. Melt some butter, stir in the sugar, almonds, sultanas and heat in a pan. Add the Tia Maria and stir well in. Then spread the mixture on top of each pancake, adding on the ice cream evenly divided and fold up the pancakes. Leave this until the very last moment otherwise your pancakes will wilt and the ice-cream will melt. If going to a restaurant, Crêpes Suzette is probably the best bet.

One final tip: the best Parfait Amour is that made by the Dutch firm, Bols.

Recipes For Scorpio

23 October — 22 November

Scorpions are passionate, secretive and very often indulgent both in food and drink. It can truly be said of them that their eyes are bigger than their tummies. What they like best are plates piled high with either Italian pasta dishes, Chinese food or curries.

Quite often they have unusual tastes in food and like experimenting. However, it pays off to ascertain quietly what these special tastes are and in what direction you can experiment: don't just risk any wildly exotic dish without making some discreet inquiries first. With Scorpions you can usually get some kind of a clue to their hidden culinary passions from learning what kind of restaurants they visit and what dishes they choose when eating out. Having made this warning, I can only add that your caution will be amply repaid by your Scorpion friend's reaction after his or her dinner.

The Scorpion's birth salt is calcium sulphate (plaster of Paris), and a deficiency of this biochemical can cause boils, ulcers, abscesses and even catarrh.

From the point of view making good any lack of calcium sulphate, Scorpions are urged to eat plenty of onions, or dishes with onions in them, cottage cheese, milk, rye bread, watercress, prunes and especially kale. The last-named is not always easy to get, but it is worth making the effort.

It is worth bearing in mind that Scorpions themselves not only like cooking, but are usually good cooks and experiment considerably in the kitchen. They will understand exactly how you have prepared a meal and instinctively know what herbs and spices you may or may not have included. They can be critical.

Thus, while you might get away with something hastily whipped up with other guests, you would be ill-advised to try a new dish for the first time with a Scorpion. He or she will know if it is a failure, while someone else – a Leonian for example – would never guess. But they do like trying out new dishes, even Japanese and Indonesian, and if you have a tested talent in this direction, it is worth giving it full rein.

Turnip and Potato Soup

Enough for 2–3 persons

Ingredients: 1¼ pints of water; ½ pint milk; 3 medium-sized peeled potatoes, cut into small pieces; 2 lbs. turnips, peeled and cut into small pieces; 1 medium-sized onion (chopped); 1 heaped tablespoon of chopped parsley and chives; 2 thin slices of bread fried in butter; salt and ground black pepper; the bottom of each soup bowl to be rubbed with a clove of garlic.

Method: Place the cut-up potatoes, turnip and chopped onion in a saucepan, add the water and cover with lid. Cook for ¾ to 1 hour on a gentle heat until tender. Then pass through a sieve or put in liquidiser; return to the saucepan, adding milk and seasoning to taste: heat to boiling point. Put the fried bread in the soup bowls, pour the soup over and sprinkle with chopped chives and parsley.

Fillet of Beef in Madeira

Enough for 2–3 persons

Ingredients: 1 lb. of fillet beef steak, trimmed; ground black pepper and salt to taste; 1 small finely chopped onion; 1 wine glass of Madeira; 1½ oz. butter; 1 level dessertspoon plain flour; 2 tablespoons of cream.

Method: Heat butter in frying pan; put in fillet steak, adding seasoning and brown all over for 5–10 minutes; then place on plate. Add chopped onion to butter in frying pan and fry gently for 5 minutes, stirring in the flour and cooking on a low heat for 1 minute. Add the wine glass of Madeira; stir until the mixture is smooth; return steak into pan with mixture and cook for a further 7–9 minutes, turning from time to time. Place steak on dish; add cream to sauce in frying pan and pour over the steak, serve immediately. French beans and sauté potatoes suggested for accompaniment.

Mixed Vegetables

Enough for 2 or 3

Ingredients: ½ lb. French beans, topped and tailed, or a packet of frozen beans; ½ lb. peeled carrots; ½ lb. peas, fresh or frozen; ¼ lb. shallots or small onions (spring onions are excellent for this purpose); 1 tablespoon butter; 1 level dessertspoon of chopped parsley.

Method: Dice carrots and beans and cut into small pieces; peel shallots or onions. Place these ingredients in a little salted, boiling water; cook until tender, but not soft, for about 7–10 minutes. Drain, melt butter in saucepan, adding vegetables. Keep on a gentle heat for 5–7 minutes, seasoning with pepper and a little salt. Place in vegetable dish and sprinkle with parsley.

Curried Eggs with Prawns

Enough for 3 persons

Ingredients: 4 hard boiled eggs; 6 oz. peeled prawns; 1 oz. plain flour; 2 oz. butter; ¾ pint milk; 1 level tablespoon curry powder; good pinch of salt; 2 tablespoons cream; 1 medium-sized onion, very finely chopped.

Method: Hard-boil the eggs for 10 minutes; place in cold water, shell and cut in half lengthwise. Put halves of eggs on dish covered with greaseproof paper in a very low oven to keep warm. Melt butter in saucepan and gently cook onion in it for 5 minutes without browning. Add flour and cook for further 1–2 minutes, without browning, stirring all the time. Add curry powder and remove from heat. Warm milk separately and pour into mixture; stir over gentle heat until thick and smooth for 5 minutes. Place eggs in fireproof dish; add prawns and cream to curry sauce; re-heat, but do not boil. Pour over eggs and serve.

Apple Purée Meringue

Enough for 2 persons

Ingredients: 1 lb. cooking apples (Bramleys for preference), peeled, cored and sliced; 3 oz. sugar; 1 oz. butter; a little water; white of 3 eggs; 3 oz. sugar.

Method: Put the peeled, cored and sliced apples in a little water in a saucepan, adding sugar, and cook gently until very soft. Then sieve, add butter and place mixture in ovenproof dish. Leave the mixture to cool and then fork up into pyramids. Whisk the egg whites until very stiff and will stand up in peaks. Add half the sugar and whisk again until smooth and white. Then fold in the remainder of the sugar. Coat the apple pyramids with the meringue mixture and place in the oven at a low heat, about 200–250 and leave to dry out for ¾–1 hour. Then serve.

Note: This is perhaps one of the bolder gambles of astrological birthday meal planning. It should work with most Scorpions. It may be, however, that your particular Scorpion has a penchant for, say, Indian and Pakistani rather than Chinese food. It would be as well to take a few soundings beforehand, but this particular menu has been designed to provide a Chinese meal for the discerning eater, one which gets away from the usual routine of "sweet and sour pork and chop suey".

The Birthday Menu

Mongolian mushroom soup with prawn crackers

Quick fried scampi with ginger, Peking style;
diced chicken and walnuts in yellow bean sauce

Barbecued spare ribs with caraway seed sauce

Fried rice with prawns, egg and green peppers
(this is often, but not always covered by the title "special fried rice")

Sweet mashed red bean pancake or toffee apples
(NB *Chinese-style* toffee-apples and NOT to be confused with the
English confection of that name)

Wine: A light white wine
(at most Chinese restaurants they usually suggest a particular
French white wine suitable for such a meal. Do not be put off if the
label bears the title "Wan Fu", or something similar, as they select
and adapt such French wines admirably)

China tea
(and you could try a glass of Sake or a Chinese liqueur, if available,
but as an optional item)

The Birthday Menu

This particular birthday meal is primarily recommended for dining out and, even then, by carefully selecting your Chinese restaurant. As a guide to where you can best obtain food of this quality, I would mention any of the Rendezvous Chinese restaurants in the London area – Soho, Gallery, Richmond, etc., the Summer Palace in Eastbourne. You could also get further advice by joining the Chinese Gourmet Club, c/o Little Gables, Bell Lane, Fetcham, Surrey.

If you do want to have this meal at home, then the best plan might be to order well in advance and arrange to take it away shortly before the actual time of your lunch or dinner. If you really want to go the whole hog and try to cook at home, then I advise that you compromise on some of the dishes. Mongolian soup is very much a regional speciality, not easily copied, and it might be sensible to substitute for this a simple sweet corn soup, either made from a packet of this genre, or by using 1 tablespoon corn oil; beaten egg whites; tin of whole sweet corn kernels; 2 pints of chicken stock (or cubes); 1 teaspoon of dry sherry (this is a substitute for rice wine); 1 tablespoon cornflour. Heat the oil in a saucepan, add the sherry, some seasoning (salt, pepper and a dash of soya sauce). Remove the sweet corn kernels from the tin and drain them, then add to the saucepan, bringing to the boil. Work in the cornflour after it has been made into a paste with a little water, stirring in. Finally add the egg whites and cook for 1 minute. Serve with prawn crackers which you can obtain from any Chinese restaurant or store, preferably warming them beforehand.

The menu presented is really a banquet-style Chinese meal and some-what too ambitious to attempt at home entirely unaided, so cut out the scampi with ginger and go for the chicken and walnuts, but omitting the yellow bean sauce. You will require: chicken breasts, enough for 2, which should be diced after lightly cooking; 4 firm pickled walnuts; a handful of split almonds (peeled); corn oil; ½ clove of garlic; 3 mush-rooms; 1 stalk of spring onion; soya sauce (you can buy this in the bottle); a pinch of powdered ginger; teaspoon of light sherry; 2 drops of sesame oil; 1 teaspoon of cornflour; 1 tablespoon of stock (chicken stock or cube); a tablespoon of sweet corn kernels; half an egg white. First of all mix together your egg white, cornflour, salt and pepper in a deep frying pan, adding the sherry and the diced chicken. Fry briefly, only until the chicken is white, avoiding any browning, and not using too much corn oil. Strain off the oil, then put in the mushrooms, which should first be sliced, the spring onion stalk cut into slivers, the pickled walnuts, garlic and sweet corn kernels. Mix together well, sprinkle with powdered ginger, add seasoning, cornflour, stock, sesame oil and a few drops of soya sauce. Re-heat and stir well, adding the almonds on top of the mixture and serve hot. The "special fried rice" may be somewhat time-consuming to make, but you can overcome this by using one of those packets of savoury rice containing green peas, red peppers, etc., and adding in pieces of prawn minutely chopped up.

This should be ample without attempting the barbecued spare ribs as well. If you are going to cook the Chinese meal yourself, I would advise, however, that you omit the spare ribs, as this dish is never quite the same when attempted by a Westerner. Substitute instead this relatively simple version of sweet and sour pork. For 2 persons you will require 2 pork cutlets, or the remains of some roast pork, if by chance you have any. Oil a deep frying pan, making the oil really hot. Meanwhile put into a saucepan, which has been very slightly oiled with corn oil, a sprinkle of salt and a clove of garlic. Warm slightly, then remove the clove of garlic and pour in 1 teacup of vinegar, 2 tablespoons of sugar, 2 teaspoons cornflour, approximately 1 tablespoon water, half a teaspoon soya sauce and pinch of pepper. Stir vigorously and heat until you have a syrupy but not too thick sauce. Cut the pork into cubes. Sprinkle with salt and pepper and coat in a mixture of flour and 2 beaten-up eggs. Then cook the meat in the boiling oil in the deep frying pan for 15 minutes. Drain off oil and then place the pork in a dish containing the sauce. Add a small quantity of sweet mixed pickles to the sauce, stirring in well. Serve with boiled rice.

Chinese Toffee apples (sometimes termed "Toffied Apples") are not too difficult to make. You will require: 2 eating apples; 2 tablespoons plain flour; 2 tablespoons water; oil for deep frying; 1 dessertspoon cornflour; 4 oz. castor sugar; 1 dessertspoon sesame seeds; 1 dessertspoon corn oil; 1 white of egg. Peel the apples and remove the cores, cut into 4 pieces, sprinkling each with a little flour. Then make a thick batter with the remaining flour, mixed with the 2 tablespoons of water, the egg white and the cornflour. Cover the pieces of apple evenly all over with this batter and deep fry very quickly in oil until the apple is a rich golden colour. Remove and drain off the fat. Meanwhile put the sugar and a little water into a small saucepan, heating and stirring until the sugar has dissolved and the mixture has boiled. Then add some corn oil, stirring again and allowing to simmer. Take the saucepan off the heat, add in the pieces of apple and the sesame seeds, turning around in the mixture for a few minutes. Plunge each toffee apple into a bowl of water and ice, then place on 2 small dishes and serve at once.

China tea is a matter of choice. It is best served in minute special Chinese teacups, unsullied either by sugar or milk, of course. If you should be able to obtain any sake, remember it is served in glasses with hot water.

Recipes For Sagittarius

23 November — 20 December

It has been said that the best thing that can happen to the Sagittarian male is that he should get married to a health food faddist. Maybe it would keep him slimmer, even remind him that one sometimes needs to think of diet. But, as a rule, the Sagittarian never thinks about such things as diet, or taking in the right amount of vitamins. He has a strong constitution, is happy-go-lucky where food is concerned and can eat almost anything.

It is more or less the same for the female, though perhaps slightly less so. She may be more inclined to watch her figure. With both sexes, luckily, their typical Sagittarian ailments have practically nothing to do with their eating, except perhaps for a tendency towards rheumatism with some of them. They are much more prone to accidents of the hips, or sprains, than to tummy troubles. Their birth salt is silica, which is to be found in the membranes covering bones, in hair, nails and skin.

Sagittarians don't have to worry unduly about how to make up for any deficiency in silica, as this biochemical is found in small quantities in several foods. Parsnips, asparagus, red cabbage, onions, Scotch oats, barley, black figs, cherries, strawberries and chicory are all silica-producing foods. And when you look closely at that list, it provides a wide range of quite attractive foods.

This sign of the zodiac is one of the Fire Signs, which also include

Aries and Leo. They all need a high protein diet. If you have a Sagittarian staying with you, you will probably find that he likes a large breakfast. This is a defence mechanism against mid-day nibbling, to which most Sagittarians and many Ariesians and Leonians for that matter are prone.

I said that Sagittarians are happy-go-lucky where food is concerned, but this should not be misconstrued into thinking they don't care what is put in front of them. They are, in fact, quite fussy in some respects and abhor anything which pretends to be a gourmet meal and is only a fifth-rate imitation of one. But they are adaptable in the sense that, if it is a party in a cellar with beer and hot sausages on skewers, they will fall in with it apparently just as enthusiastically as if it was a five-course sit-down banquet in a five-star hotel. But they could get bored if offered the same fare night after night.

Indeed, the clue to the Sagittarian is that he loves travel. Not only will he go a long way for a really good meal, but he will go a long way just to escape from a bad one. He would, however, be furious if, at the end of his journey, he found he was disappointed. This goes for Ms. Sagittarius, too. As travellers, Sagittarians believe very much in eating the food of the country they are visiting; they delight in trying out new dishes, though not always with the same abandon as Scorpio.

Roast Duck with Pineapple and Mushrooms

Enough for 4 persons

Ingredients: 1 fresh duck, 4 to 5 lb., already dressed; 8 oz. button mushrooms, cleaned and left whole; half a fresh pineapple, peeled and cut into neat chunks (you could use tinned pineapple, preferably the rings and not the chunks); 5 tablespoons kirsch; 4 tablespoons fresh cream; 1 level dessertspoon plain flour; 2 oz. butter; salt and ground black pepper to taste; a small onion.

Method: Wipe the duck with a damp cloth and remove any interior excess fat. Rub duck all over with salt and prick with a fork. Then place the duck in a roasting pan on a wire rack. Cook in a moderate oven for 1½–2 hours, allowing 30 minutes per lb. and 25 minutes over this time. Cook the giblets in a saucepan with a small onion for 1½ hours. Soak the peeled and chunked pineapple in 3 tablespoons of kirsch for 1½ hours. Melt butter in saucepan, add plain flour, and stir until lightly browned; add ½ pint of giblet stock and cook gently for 5 minutes. Next lightly cook the whole button mushrooms in a little butter for 5 minutes, afterwards adding to the sauce in the saucepan. Remove the pineapple from the kirsch and add to the sauce and the mushrooms. Heat the remainder of the kirsch in a very small saucepan, meanwhile removing the duck from the oven. Pour the kirsch over the duck and light with a match. Then remove the excess duck fat from the roasting pan and pour the duck juices into the pineapple and mushroom sauce. Place the duck on a dish. Add cream to the sauce and also any remaining kirsch: re-heat, but do not allow to boil. Pour the sauce around the duck and serve. The duck may be cut into portions, or left whole. Garnish with sprigs of parsley.

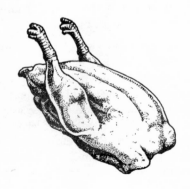

Endive au Gratin

Enough for 2–3 persons

Ingredients: 4 chicories (well rounded); 4 slices of lean ham; 3 ozs. grated Gruyère cheese and 1 oz. Parmesan cheese, mixed together; 1 oz. plain flour; 2½ oz. butter; ½ pint milk; 2 tablespoons cream; ½ teaspoon nutmeg; ground black pepper to taste.

Method: Wipe the chicory with a damp cloth, slice a thin piece off the bottom end of each chicory where there is likely to be slight discoloration. Blanch the chicory in boiling water for 10–15 minutes; then drain well, and leave to cool. Wrap each chicory in ham and place in oven-proof dish. Melt 1½ oz. butter in a saucepan, add flour and cook gently for a minute. Heat the milk and pour into the butter and flour mixture, stirring all the time until the mixture is thick and smooth. Add 2 oz. of mixed cheese and cream, with seasoning to taste and nutmeg. Pour the sauce over the chicory; sprinkle on the rest of the cheese and dot with the rest of the butter. Place in oven and cook for 25–30 minutes until golden brown on top. Serve with lettuce salad, dressed with oil and vinegar.

Stuffed Cos Lettuce

Enough for 2–3

Ingredients: 2 cos lettuces, cut in halves, lengthwise and well washed; 1 medium-sized onion, chopped; 3 oz. long-grained, cooked rice; 4 oz. button mushrooms wiped with damp cloth and thinly sliced; 6 oz. minced veal, chicken or pork (left-overs can be used); 1 hard-boiled egg, chopped; 1 teaspoon chopped parsley; 1 teaspoon chopped basil (or dried basil soaked in a little boiling water); salt and pepper to taste; ½ teaspoon cinnamon; 1 wineglass white wine or dry cider; 3 oz. butter.

Method: Place lettuce halves in enough cold water just to cover; bring to the boil, blanching for 2–3 minutes. Drain thoroughly, put two of the halves of lettuce in a buttered ovenproof dish, flat sides up. Melt 2 oz . of the butter in a saucepan and gently cook the mushrooms, onion and mince for 5–7 minutes; add the rice and all the other ingredients, and wine. Fill two of the halves of lettuce with the stuffing and cover with the other two. Pour the melted butter over both lettuces and cook in a moderate oven for 1 hour, covering the dish with grease-proof paper.

Canterbury Soup

Enough for 2–3 persons

Ingredients: 1 lb. ripe tomatoes, peeled and cut into slices; ½ lb. potatoes, peeled and cut into small pieces; 2 small leeks, washed and chopped up; 2 sticks of celery, washed and cut into small pieces; 1 dessertspoon chopped chervil; 1 level teaspoon powdered bayleaf; 3 oz. butter; seasoning to taste, salt and pepper; 1½ pints water or stock.

Method: Cook tomatoes in melted butter in a saucepan for 7 minutes, adding all other ingredients and cooking for a further 7 minutes with the lid on. Add water, bring to boil, and simmer gently for 45–50 minutes. Pass through a sieve, return soup to saucepan, re-heat and serve.

Charlotte Royal

Enough for 3–4

Ingredients: ½ cup of sugar; pinch of salt; 2 egg yolks; 2 egg whites beaten stiff; grated rind and juice of a medium-sized lemon; ½ cup of a Muscatel wine; 1 cup of double cream; 1 level dessertspoon gelatine; 1 packet of sponge fingers; 6 glacé cherries; 6 fresh strawberries; some toasted, split almonds.

Method: Mix the sugar, salt, egg yolks, grated rind and juice of lemon and the Muscatel wine in a large bowl. Place the bowl over a saucepan of boiling water. Beat with a rotary whisk over the heat until thick and frothy. Dissolve the gelatine in a little water in a small basin over a small saucepan of hot water. Add the gelatine to the mixture and leave to cool, but not to set. Whisk the egg whites to a snow-like texture and whip the cream. Cut a small piece of sponge off one tip of each of the sponge fingers to enable them to be stood up and arranged around a glass mould. If you have difficulty in making them stand up, a little jam (say strawberry or similar) smeared on the ends where the pieces have been cut off will often do the trick. Fold into the mixture with alternative spoonfuls of each the egg whites and whipped cream. Pour the mixture into the mould; put into the refrigerator and leave to set. Decorate with cherries, strawberries and a little whipped cream and sprinkle with toasted almonds. If you can't get fresh strawberries at this time of the year (in large cities it should not be too difficult), then substitute any other fresh fruit to your taste, or glacé cherries and angelica.

The Birthday Menu

Moussaka

Venison Cutlets

Melon with grapes soaked in
anis liqueur
(or crême de menthe)

Coffee & Remy Martin brandy

Wine: Château Neuf du Pape

The Birthday Menu

For the moussaka you will require (for 2 persons): 1 lb. of aubergines (peeled or unpeeled), cubed and parboiled briefly. Drain thoroughly, place in a buttered casserole. Then take ½ lb. of minced beef which you brown in a skillet. Add to this half a small tin of tomato paste and an equal amount of water, salt, pepper, thyme and a little sugar. Cook until the meat is well coated and not too soupy. A small quantity of chopped up onion and mushrooms can be added after browning in butter. This mixture should then be put over the aubergines in the casserole. Finally, pour over the whole a Béchamel sauce – simply made by melting 2 oz. butter and adding in 1 oz. flour and half a pint of milk, stirring and heating). Sprinkle liberally with grated cheese and, if you wish, paprika. Bake in a moderate oven for half an hour, then serve.

If you decide to take Sagittarius out to a restaurant, it might be worth while altering the second course to venison braised in red wine sauce. But the venison cutlets are more suited for a *tete a tete* at home. Choose the best end of the neck of venison for the cutlets; you will also require 2 oz. butter, ½ lb. mushrooms, ¼ pint of good brown stock (or cube); pepper and salt. Skin and trim the mushrooms and then stew them slowly in a saucepan with stock, butter, seasoning and (if you wish) a handful of mixed herbs, for 30–35 minutes. Cut up the venison into cutlets, having trimmed off the bone; smear them with melted butter, adding salt and pepper, and then grill for about 20 minutes. Serve with the stewed mushrooms and red currant jelly. For additional vegetables you can have green beans and potato rissoles.

For the dessert choose a very ripe melon and cut into quarters, or halves if a small melon. Carve out the seed and pulp. Take a quantity of sweet white grapes, slit open slightly so that you can remove the pips and insert some anis liqueur. Having done this put all the grapes into a small glass dish containing the rest of the anis liqueur and turn the grapes around until they are well impregnated with the liqueur. Finally, place an equal quantity of grapes in each section of melon.

Recipes For Capricorn

21 December — 19 January

Capricornians are persevering, ambitious types who like good things, but are rather cautious and conservative in their approach to food. They are not exactly mean, for they will spend freely on good things, but they have a passion for being economical, for making things last and for getting the best value out of their shopping and their cooking.

In their daily life they like the minimum of fuss and tend to go for meals which are quickly and economically prepared. They will especially admire a meal of good, solid, plain food without unnecessary trimmings. They themselves can conjure culinary miracles out of the scantiest material.

The birth salt of Capricorn is calcium phosphate. Lack of this constituent can create havoc in the digestive juices, intestinal ailments and even rheumatism. Calcium phosphate can be taken in tablet form, but is, as we have seen with Cancerians and Scorpions, to be found in cottage cheese, wholemeal bread and onions – an excellent mixture for Capricornians – and in leeks, prunes, cabbage and milk and carrot juice.

However, important though such foods may be to the well-being of the Capricornian, he is far from being a faddist and is not as a rule a health-product addict. To please the Capricornian of either sex the emphasis should be on the dish that fills – on roast joints, Virginian hams and, if venturing into the field of foreign cooking, go for the substantial Middle European or Hungarian rather than the epicurean delights of France. Even then you should avoid too many frills, or unusual sauces.

This may sound as though with the Capricornian you have to be over-watchful. Not to worry, this sign of the zodiac may be characterised by caution, conservatism and a reluctance to make eating the kind of adventure which it often is for a Sagittarian, but, once won over, the Capricornian is reliable, a loyal friend, punctual and always remembers a good turn.

One point to note is that Capricornians are not easily fobbed off by substitutes; they like the unusual when it really is the best of its kind. An imitation caviar is not for them, though the real thing with blinis they would probably accept readily.

Cucumber Salad

Enough for 2 persons
Ingredients: 1 cucumber, peeled and thinly sliced; 2 tomatoes, thinly sliced; a few leaves of young lettuce; 2 tablespoons olive oil; 1 dessertspoon wine vinegar; ground black pepper and salt to taste; 1 small finely chopped onion; 1 level dessertspoon of chopped tarragon.

Method: Place peeled, sliced cucumber on plate and add a little salt. Leave this on one side for $\frac{1}{2}$ hour, then wash under cold water and drain well. Mix oil, vinegar, seasoning and onion together, thoroughly stirring. Then pour over the cucumber and allow to settle for 1–2 hours. Add sliced tomatoes, place on bed of lettuce leaves and sprinkle with chopped tarragon. Then serve.

Rings of Marrow Stuffed with Salmon

Enough for 3 persons

Ingredients: 4 small knobs of butter; 1 medium-sized young marrow; 8 oz. tin of red salmon, or fresh cooked salmon; 1 dessertspoon chopped green olives; 1 dessertspoon tomato purée; freshly ground black pepper and salt to taste; 2 tablespoons double cream; 4 chopped anchovies.

Method: Peel the young marrow and cut into two-inch slices, scooping out all the seeds, having first cut off thin slices at each end of marrow. Place the salmon in a bowl, having removed the skin and bones (and oil, if tinned). Take care not to turn this into a paste, but flake up the salmon with a fork. Add chopped olives, anchovies, seasoning, tomato purée and cream and mix all well together. Fill each of the marrow rings with the salmon mixture and put a knob of butter on each ring. Grease a shallow oven-proof dish and put the stuffed rings in it. Place in a pre-heated oven at about 350°; cover with foil or grease-proof paper and bake the marrow-rings in the oven for 35–40 minutes. Serve hot with lettuce salad, oil and vinegar.

Partridge on Canape

Enough for 2 persons

Ingredients: 1 partridge; 2 slices of white bread fried in fat from the partridge; liver of the partridge, cooked and crushed with a fork; white breadcrumbs; 2 oz. butter; 1 slice of fat bacon; some flour.

Method: Take one young partridge which has been plucked and trussed; cover the breast with bacon, which you attach to the bird with cotton. Cook in a pre-heated, moderate oven for 30–35 minutes, basting with melted butter several times during the cooking. Shortly before serving remove the bacon, and sprinkle a little flour over the breast, then baste and cook until golden brown, after which the partridge should be placed on a dish. Meantine stew the liver of the partridge for 5–8 minutes and mash into a pulp with a fork. Put fat from the partridge into a frying pan in which you fry the white bread, after the crusts have been removed. Fry on both sides. Spread the mashed liver on the pieces of fried bread; cut the partridge in half lengthwise and place a half on each piece of fried bread. Serve immediately with chips and peas or Brussels sprouts. You will find this makes a delicious meal without any sauces or other additions.

Coffee Ice-Cream with Grand Marnier

Enough for 4 persons

Ingredients: 1 packet of coffee ice-cream, or home-made; 5 oz. double cream, whipped; 1 wine glass of Grand Marnier; 1 oz. chopped, toasted almonds; 1½ oz. preserved ginger, roughly chopped into small pieces; 4 glacé cherries.

Method: Mix the ice-cream with the chopped pieces of preserved ginger and fill a glass or other bowl with the mixture. Put in freezer compartment of refrigerator until well set and solid. Then fill 4 silver ice-cream cups, or 4 tall-stemmed glasses, with equal amounts of the mixture, up to about ¾ full. Pour equal amounts of Grand Marnier into each glass over each portion of ice-cream. Add the whipped cream to each glass and top with a glacé cherry and toasted almonds. Serve immediately.

Savoury Mushrooms

Enough for 2 persons

Ingredients: 4 large open mushrooms; 2 oz. grated Gruyère cheese; 1 medium-sized chopped onion; 1 dessertspoon chopped parsley; ground black pepper and salt to taste; ½ teaspoon paprika; 2 level dessertspoons fresh breadcrumbs; ½ teaspoon ground mace; 2 oz. butter.

Method: Peel the mushrooms, removing the stalks and wipe with a damp cloth. Place in a shallow, greased oven-proof dish. Sprinkle with the pepper, salt (remember the cheese will be salty, so go easy with the salt), mace, paprika, chopped onion and parsley. Mix well together the cheese and breadcrumbs. Fill the mushrooms with this mixture and dot with knobs of butter. Then cook in pre-heated moderate oven for 20 minutes. Serve hot.

The Birthday Menu

Smoked salmon cornets stuffed with
fresh prawns and a brandy sauce

Pork chops cooked in Madeira

Zabaglione

Coffee: note that the odds are your
Capricornian will not want a liqueur

Wine: Ideally, a half bottle of a Chablis and a
half bottle of Rosé (for 2), or a full bottle of Rosé

The Birthday Menu

This is not too difficult a meal to attempt at home. Possibly the most difficult item is the *hors d'oeuvre*. The cornets you require are very similar to those of the ice-cream variety: indeed, you can use just those. Roll your slices of smoked salmon round the fresh prawns and fill the cornets with them. Some restaurateurs conjure up a very special brandy sauce with this dish, but you can effectively obtain the same results with a sauce of hot melted butter thickened with a spoonful of flour, to which is added finely shredded fresh prawns, a dash of lemon juice and a tablespoon of brandy, mixed in a saucepan.

For the pork chops dish you will require 4 or 6 small, lean chops; 1 large onion cut into small pieces; salt and pepper, 1½ tablespoons of flour; 1 bay leaf; 2 tablespoons sour cream; 2 tablespoons Madeira (you can use more to taste, if you wish). First trim the chops, removing all the fat, putting the trimmings into a saucepan with just enough water to cover. Boil for at least an hour. Fry the chops slowly in a pan. Put the finely sliced onion (this can be sieved) into the saucepan with the trimmings, add the flour, and stir. Add the Madeira, bay leaf and salt and pepper. The sauce must be thick enough to coat the chops (you can add gelatine, if you wish). Serve the chops in a dish, surrounding with peas (or green beans) and sliced carrot, and pour the sauce over them.

Zabaglione is fairly easy to make, but it must be left until the last minute. You will require for 2 persons: 3 egg yolks, 4 teaspoons Marsala wine; 3 teaspoons sugar. Put the egg yolks in a saucepan over simmering water (using a double-boiler is the best method, otherwise a smaller saucepan placed inside a larger one containing the simmering water). Whisk the yolks, adding in the Marsala and the sugar, stirring all the time. Keep stirring until the mixture is thick and frothy, then pour into glasses and serve at once.

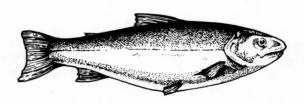

Recipes For Aquarius

20 January — 18 February

"An Aquarian? Ah, now there goes someone rather special," you may hear people say. And on the whole this is so; the typical Aquarian is intensely individualistic, revelling in freedom, original and sometimes contrary just for the sake of being different.

But Aquarians love people and so they delight in going out to dine and being entertained. And there is the added bonus that they generally equally like returning the entertainment. Often highly strung, with their weak points being their nervous system, circulation, legs and ankles, they tend to pay serious attention to their diet and what they should and should not eat, because experience has taught them that this is their wisest course.

There is a marked link between the nervous and digestive systems with Aquarians and this is one reason why they often go on prolonged slimming diets, or indulge in macrobiotic diets. Nevertheless, they also love the luxuries of the *bonne cuisine* and the carefully chosen wine cellar. So you must be prepared for any of two moods with almost all Aquarians – the plain, simple salad or the carefully prepared special meal.

With regard to the latter, it is as well to note that even when it comes to luxury foods, the Aquarian retains a watchful eye on health and diet. Not for her fried scampi, but a grilled Dover sole. The female Aquarian seems to avoid fried food and much prefers grills or even steamed dishes.

The Aquarian's birth salt is sodium chloride, or what is more usually called common salt. And therein lies a problem for making up any salt deficiency. You cannot compensate for a lack of salt by taking common salt; the body doesn't easily absorb it and excessive use of salt could lead to high blood pressure, hardening of the arteries and even some skin diseases.

Sodium chloride must be introduced into the system by salads, fruits and other foodstuffs. Salads comprising spinach leaves, radishes and slices of orange and lemon are excellent. So, too, are baked apples in various forms and celery either cooked, raw, or in soups.

Calves' Kidneys and Mushrooms, Flambé in Brandy

Enough for 2–3 persons

Ingredients: 2 medium-size calves' kidneys (or 6 fresh lambs' kidneys); 4 oz. butter; 6 oz. button mushrooms, cleaned and sliced; 1 teaspoon lemon juice; ground black pepper and salt to taste; 1 dessertspoon chopped parsley; 1 small onion, finely chopped; 1 wine-glass of brandy; 1–2 tablespoons of stock (note this latter item is optional).

Method: Remove the skins from the kidneys, cut in halves, lengthwise. Then remove core and cut into small pieces. Melt 2 oz. butter in a frying pan and gently cook the chopped onion for about 6–7 minutes, until tender and without browning. Add the kidneys to the pan and cook rapidly for 4–5 minutes; then remove from the heat. In another pan melt the remainder of the butter, add the mushrooms and cook gently for 4–6 minutes. Then re-heat the kidneys, meanwhile heating the brandy in a saucepan. Pour the heated brandy over the kidneys and light with a match. You can, if you wish, add one or two tablespoons of stock to the mushrooms, which should be added to the kidneys, mixed together and served on a heated dish. Sprinkle with the chopped parsley.

Salsify with Cream

Enough for 2 or 3 persons

Ingredients: 1 lb. of salsify (pronounced as spelt in Anglo-Saxon territories, but salsifis (sal-si-fee) if on the continent); 5oz. carton of cream; ground black pepper and salt to taste; 1 tablespoon lemon juice; 1 tablespoon chopped parsley and chives.

Method: Wash the salsify well, then scrape or thinly peel and cut into 3-inch pieces. Put in a saucepan of cold water with the lemon juice and salt and simmer for 1½ hours, or until tender. Drain the salsify and then return to the saucepan. Pour the cream over the salsify and cook gently for 10–15 minutes until the cream is reduced to half the quantity. Then place in a hot dish and sprinkle all over with the chopped parsley and chives and serve.

Apricot Soufflé

Enough for 3–4 persons

Ingredients: 1 lb. fresh apricots (or 14 oz. dried apricots which have been soaked in water and cooked in the usual way first); 2 tablespoons castor sugar; 1½ oz. powdered gelatine; 5 oz. carton of double or whipping cream; 3 large egg whites; 1 heaped tablespoon of equal quantities of finely chopped almonds and walnuts; 4 glacé cherries; 4 halves of apricots (i.e. apricots cut in half); 5 tablespoons hot water; 1 tablespoon lemon juice.

Method: Attach to the outside of a soufflé dish a double thickness of greaseproof paper or foil. Cook the stoned apricots and sugar (retaining the 4 halves) in a saucepan, after which drain and leave to cool. When the apricots are completely cool, sieve or liquidise; pour into a large bowl. Dissolve the powdered gelatine in the hot water in a small basin over a saucepan of boiling water until completely dissolved. Whisk the cream with a rotary whisk and add lemon juice to apricots. Then whisk the whites of the eggs until they are stiff and standing up in pyramidical peaks. Gently fold the egg whites and cream into the sieved apricots. Put half the ingredients into the soufflé dish; then sprinkle half the chopped nuts on to the soufflé, adding the remainder of the soufflé mixture. Place in the refrigerator and leave to set. Remove the greaseproof paper (or foil) from the soufflé dish, decorate the whole with glacé cherries and the 4 halves of apricot and sprinkle with the remaining nuts.

Stuffed Cabbage

Enough for 2–3 persons

Ingredients: 3 small cabbages, washed and cleaned; ¾ lb. of equal parts of minced beef, veal and pork (or any left-overs of meat); 1 medium-sized chopped onion; 1 tablespoon tomato purée; ½ level teaspoon of curry powder, powdered mace and mixed herbs; 1 clove of crushed garlic (optional); ground black pepper and salt to taste; 1 level teaspoon of plain flour; 2 tablespoons of white wine, or a dry, strong cider (if available); 3 tablespoons of sunflower seed oil; 2½ oz. grated Gruyère cheese.

Method: Clean the cabbages thoroughly, cut into halves lengthwise, place in boiling salted water and blanch for 5 minutes. Drain well and leave to cool. Heat the oil in a saucepan and in it gently fry the onions without browning. Add the meat and garlic and cook with the onions for a further 6 minutes, stirring well with a wooden spoon. Then add the tomato purée, curry powder, mace, herbs and flour, stirring all the time: add the wine or cider and cook for 5 minutes. Place a tablespoon of the stuffing between the leaves of the halves of cabbage, gently press down the leaves and re-shape. Place the cabbage halves, flat sides down, in a greased oven-proof dish and sprinkle the top of each with the grated cheese. Cover with foil and place in a moderate oven for 20–30 minutes. Serve with grated carrot salad and chopped watercress.

Caramelled Carrots

Enough for 2–3 persons

Ingredients: 1 lb. carrots, peeled or scraped (essentially new carrots); 1½ oz. castor sugar; 1½ oz. butter; 1 dessertspoon grated nutmeg (optional); pepper to taste; 1 oz. finely chopped, blanched almonds; a little salt.

Method: Clean the carrots and boil in salted water until tender, but not soft. Drain off the water. Melt butter in a saucepan, add sugar and water and slowly bring to the boil, stirring all the time. When mixture is thickened and lightly brown, add the carrots and continue to cook on a very low heat with the lid on for about 5 minutes, shaking the saucepan from time to time to coat the carrots. Place in a hot dish and sprinkle with chopped almonds.

The Birthday Menu

Consommé

Grilled Dover Sole
and lettuce salad

Rum-baked banana & cream

Coffee and Yellow Chartreuse

Wine: A good Montrachet white,
preferably a Bâtard Montrachet

The Birthday Menu

Today it is simplest (especially when catering for two) to produce consommé out of a tin. There is a wide variety of tinned consommé available. The problem, when making consommé yourself, is the time it takes. With some soups this can be anything from 2 to 6 hours, or even more! But you can make a clear soup that takes as short a time as half an hour or an hour. The half-hour soup is one made of vermi-celli (adding this to $1\frac{1}{2}$ pints of a clear soup from a tin or stock). Or you can use $1\frac{1}{2}$ pints of unclarified stock, adding in such extras as a bouquet-garni of mixed herbs, thyme, bayleaf, a few green peas, asparagus tops, sliced onion and carrot. You cook your vegetables first, dice them, and then add to the stock, which should already have been heated and flavoured with the onion and herbs.

The grilled Dover sole can be cooked in exactly the same way as for the Cancer birthday menu. The only difference is that this time it will be served with a crisp lettuce salad, to which can be added slices of lemon, finely sliced tomatoes and cucumber.

The dessert should be quite simply made by lightly cooking the sliced bananas in rum and butter in a frying pan. You can, if you wish, add a few sliced glacé cherries and sultanas. Pour the rum sauce over the bananas and serve with cream.

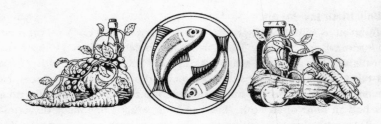

Recipes For Pisces

19 February — 20 March

Pisceans, like Cancerians (and to a lesser extent Scorpions), are very fond of fish, but often without knowing it they are allergic to it. Or rather, they are allergic to certain fish. With Pisceans oysters, mussels and some shellfish can produce stomach pains and sickness.

But fish with the Piscean is very much hit and miss. What may go down splendidly one day will be disastrous another. Even grilled sole, normally a safe dish, can induce that allergy in a Piscean. So don't take the sign of the fish as a go-ahead for any fish dish when entertaining Pisceans. Yet they do adore fish, so you must do your homework and find out what's what.

Their birth salt is iron phosphate and it is worth recalling that when iron is lacking in the system there is a risk of anaemia. A deficiency of iron phosphate in the Piscean causes a risk of a number of ailments including palpitations of the heart, headaches, insomnia and even nervous upsets. It is probably true to say that Pisceans need to pay greater attention to any lack of their birth salt than people of any other sign of the zodiac.

So top of the list for the Pisces character must be foods containing iron and the vegetables among these should be eaten raw where possible. Vital foodstuffs for Pisces are cereals, root vegetables, spinach, beans, lettuce, peas, nuts, raisins, dates, figs and prunes.

Pisceans are apt to be romanticists and nowhere does this trait reveal itself more than in their kitchens. They like to serve up imaginative and original snacks at parties and, when being entertained, expect their own hospitality to be adequately reciprocated. They are themselves prone to overspend in order to have the kind of meals they like. You won't go far with a Piscean by taking her out for a Welsh rarebit and a cup of coffee, or by inviting him to take pot luck at your home with a re-heated mince of the day before.

Raw vegetables in salads suit them admirably, though when being entertained they may wish for richer fare. They love beef Bourguignonne, grilled trout with almonds (make sure this is not a hidden allergy, if you can!), duck cooked with oranges and rice dishes. On the whole, they are not too difficult to cater for as they have catholic tastes in food.

Chicken Veronique

Enough for 3 persons

Ingredients: 1 small fresh chicken cut into 4 pieces (or chicken joints); 1 glass of white wine; ½ pint of stock (or chicken cube); ground black pepper and salt to taste; ¼ pint of cream; 3 oz. of sweet, white grapes (if possible seedless); 1 oz. plain flour; 1 oz. butter; 6 triangles of puff pastry, or fried croutons; 1 carrot; 1 onion; bayleaf; thyme.

Method: Gently cook the pieces of chicken in the stock (or using the cube to make stock) until tender, for about ½ an hour. Take out of the pan and remove all the skin and bones from the chicken. Place in an oven-proof dish and cover with foil; then keep hot in a low oven. Melt the butter, add flour and cook for 2 minutes, stirring all the time, gradually pouring in the chicken stock and white wine, seasoning to taste. Slowly bring to the boil and then cook gently for 3 minutes until the mixture is thick. Remove the pan from the heat, add cream, stir and then re-heat, but do not allow to boil again. Pour the mixture over the chicken, add the grapes and decorate with baked puff pastry triangles, or croutons, and then serve immediately.

91

Coquilles Saint Jacques au Gratin

Enough for 2 or 4 persons, according to whether you make this a "starter" or a main course

Ingredients: 4 scallops in their shells and taking care to retain the shells; 3 oz. butter; 1 oz. plain flour; 1 wine glass of white wine; yolk of 1 egg; 4 oz. button mushrooms sliced; ground black pepper and salt to taste; 1 medium-sized onion or 3 shallots; 2–3 oz. white breadcrumbs; 1 dessertspoon lemon juice.

Method: Pisceans usually adore anything in the nature of Coquilles St. Jacques and there are, of course, several versions of this dish, some more varied and exotic than others. Bearing in mind both the Piscean's love of fish and the allergy of some of them to certain types of fish, I have omitted mussels, prawns etc. from this dish and aimed at something essentially simple, but inviting. First, ask your fishmonger to clean the scallops for you. Wash the shells and retain for use as receptacles for the completed dish. Make a stock by putting a bayleaf, a small onion, thyme, parsley, a clove of garlic and a piece of carrot in a piece of muslin and placing in a saucepan of cold water; bring to the boil, then simmer for 20 minutes, adding salt to taste. Wash the scallops and put them in the stock for 5–6 minutes. Melt some butter, adding to it the chopped onion and sliced mushrooms; then cook for 5 minutes without browning. Melt the remaining butter in a small saucepan; add flour and cook for 3–4 minutes, stirring continuously until a golden brown colour. Slowly add the wine and, if judged necessary, a little of the stock in which the scallops were cooked. Stir continuously and cook for 3 minutes, allowing to cool slightly before adding the egg yolk. Mix well, add the mushrooms and chopped onions and then the scallops. Place equal portions of this mixture in each scallop shell, covering with breadcrumbs. Add a small knob of butter to each scallop shell and cook in a moderate oven for 15 minutes.

Banana Benedictine

Enough for 2–3 persons

Ingredients: 4 medium-sized bananas; 1 tablespoon Benedictine; 1 tablespoon brandy; juice of half an orange; grated rind of half a lemon; grated rind of half an orange; juice of half a small lemon; 1½ oz. butter; 1½ oz. sugar; 3 oz. Morella cherries; 1 oz. chopped and blanched almonds.

Method: Melt butter in a frying pan, add the juices and grated rinds of orange and lemon and sugar; bring to the boil. Cut the bananas in halves lengthwise and add to the mixture, cooking until just tender, but still firm. Add the Benedictine and brandy and the Morella cherries (which have previously been de-frozen), cooking for 2 minutes and turning all the time to heat evenly. Place on a hot dish and sprinkle with chopped almonds.

Apple and Cucumber Salad

Enough for 3–4 persons

Ingredients: 1 medium cucumber, thinly sliced; 2 eating apples, thinly sliced; 5 oz. carton of soured cream; 1 dessertspoon lemon juice; ground black pepper and salt to taste; 6 spring onions chopped; 1 oz. chopped walnuts.

Method: Peel the apples and cucumber and then slice into thin pieces. Sprinkle with lemon juice, pepper and salt and mix thoroughly. Add chopped onions to soured cream, mixing well together, and then pour over the apple and cucumber. Place the whole mixture in a salad bowl and sprinkle with walnuts.

Onion Soup

Enough for 2–3 persons

Ingredients: ½ lb. onions; 2 pints of stock (or cube of vegetable stock); 3 oz. butter; 1½ oz. flour; salt and pepper to taste; 1 clove of garlic; grated Parmesan cheese; 1 slice of buttered bread for each soup bowl.

Method: Peel the onions and roughly chop into pieces rather than slices. Melt the butter in a saucepan, add the onions and cook until they are a golden brown. Add flour and allow to brown, cooking for 10–15 minutes in the vegetable stock. Put the pieces of buttered bread in the soup bowls and pour the soup over them. Serve immediately with a dish of Parmesan cheese to sprinkle on.

The Birthday Menu

Shrimp à la Kraft or
Whitebait

Canard aux oranges
(duck cooked with oranges and an orange sauce; there
are various versions of this, but for a Piscean you should
ensure that the duck is well chosen and well cooked:
a bad *canard aux oranges* can be disastrous)

Hot baked Grapefruit
Hawaii topped with cinnamon

Coffee and Green Chartreuse

Wine: Domaine de Voujon
or a Macôn

The Birthday Menu

Pisceans are much more a hit and miss type than those of other signs of the zodiac and this is particularly true of Pisceans near the cusp. It is for this reason that alternative dishes are offered for a starter. Shrimp à la Kraft's origin is somewhat of a mystery: this recipe comes from a friend in Texas. You require (for 2 persons) 2 dessertspoons of butter; $2\frac{1}{2}$ dessertspoons of flour; 1 cup of milk, all of which you mix together first to make the sauce. To this you add a quarter of a green pepper (slivered), quarter of a pimento; 1 cup of shrimps; half a teaspoon of Worcester sauce and half a teaspoon of mayonnaise. When hot, serve at once in toast cups placed on a large dish. To make toast cups, you slice the crusts off square pieces of bread, thinly cut; toast the bread, then, while still hot, put the pieces of toast into small glass dishes, pressing them down hard so that they take the exact shape of the mould. When the toast is cold, remove the toast cups from the glasses and fill with the mixture.

If you go for whitebait instead, you simply require whitebait, pepper, salt and frying fat or oil. It sounds simple, but the truth is that whitebait is best left for a professional cook unless you have real flair. Sprinkle the fish with flour and cook in a wire basket, which should be plunged into a deep pan of very hot oil or fat. Fry on a high heat for about 4–5 minutes. Keep moving the basket all the time and, when you remove from the heat, shake it to get rid of the oil. The fish should be placed on kitchen paper or a cloth until all fat is strained off. Then serve on a very hot dish with slices of lemon and slices of brown bread and butter.

For *canard aux oranges* you will require: 1 fresh duck (*not* frozen) about 4–6 lb.; 1 wine glass of curacoa; 2 oz. butter; 1oz. plain flour; 3 oranges; 1 cup of stock; the liver of the duck; salt and pepper to taste. Cooking time for the duck should be at the rate of 20 minutes per pound, with 25 minutes over. First peel one orange very thinly. Then remove the pith from the orange; cut into pieces and place inside the duck. Chop up the peel of the orange and keep until later. Prick the skin of the duck with a fork, place it in the roasting dish in a hot oven, say 450° electric, reducing the heat eventually to 350°. Twenty minutes before the duck is cooked make the following sauce: cook the chopped orange peel for 10 minutes in a little boiling water, strain, crush very finely the orange peel and the duck's liver together, adding the curacoa. Place in a small saucepan the stock (veal stock for preference, or a chicken cube); mix together the flour and butter into a paste, add the liver and orange peel, stirring all the time, add the stock to these ingredients and return to the saucepan; bring to the boil, stirring continuously for 3 minutes. Then pass through sieve or liquidiser and re-heat. Cut the remaining oranges into quarters or slices and arrange around a hot dish. Remove the duck from the oven, strain off all fat and pour the juices from the duck into the sauce. Place the duck on the hot dish with the orange slices, putting a tablespoon of the sauce over the duck and the remainder in a sauce boat. Serve immediately: suggest green peas and game chips as accompaniment.

If you have any doubts about the *canard aux oranges*, when going out to a restaurant, then switch your choice to *Poulet Marengo*, that dish which originated on the battlefield of Marengo when Napoleon sent his chefs out scavenging for chicken and titbits which Napoleon's chefs never found, but, never mind, most Pisceans will wallow in the romance of it all. Mug up your history to build a story around the dish, if he or she has never heard of it. When Napoleon won the battle, he wanted a celebratory dinner so his chefs were instructed to scour the surrounding countryside. Chicken, mushrooms, eggs and vegetables they may well have found, but it seems very doubtful that they were lucky enough to come up with shrimps and mussels as well – ingredients which are sometimes included in *Poulet Marengo*.

The Hot Baked Grapefruit Hawaii is quite simple to make. Prepare your grapefruit in two halves, slicing around the inner edge of the peel to separate the fruit and then cutting segments from the middle outwards, but leaving the loosened pieces in their respective peel. Place on top of each half glacé cherries, sultanas and split, peeled almonds. Pour on a little liquid honey and sprinkle with demerara sugar and place under the grill for a few minutes. Take care not to burn and then serve piping hot.

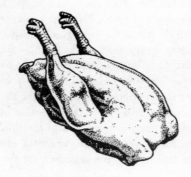

Drinking around the Zodiac

"What does drink effect? It unlocks secrets; bids our hopes to be realised; urges the dastard to the fight; lifts the load from troubled minds; teaches accomplishments."

So said Horace, writing in the first century B.C., and ever since then poets and romantics of every kind have paid tribute to the elusive magic of alcoholic beverages. It is, perhaps, unusual for a cookery book to include an appendix on drinks, yet there is every reason why one should. You can prepare or plan the most splendid meal, yet all can be ruined if due attention is not paid not only to what you drink with it, but to what you sip before and after.

In the menus proffered for each sign of the zodiac suggestions have been made as to what should be drunk with the meals. It should be stressed that these suggestions are based primarily on what wines go with which dishes. On the other hand some attention has been paid to the known likes and dislikes of Ariesians, Taurians, Geminians, etc.

Generally speaking, all you have to do when choosing a birthday meal is to settle for a wine that goes with the main course. The norm should be a bottle of wine between two people, but in some cases a half bottle will suffice. Leonians, it should be noted, do not as a rule take kindly to sharing a half bottle. They much prefer a full bottle of a cheaper wine than a half bottle of something more expensive.

Sometimes, as in the case of the menu chosen for Capricorn, the first course strictly requires a white wine and the main course a red. You can compromise, as I have suggested, by serving a rosé, but this might not suit a perfectionist such as Capricornians can occasionally be. So the answer is for half a bottle of white and another half of red.

Champagne appeals to those born under certain signs of the zodiac. This is one of the few firm astrological associations between birth signs and wine. Gemini has been specially selected for a champagne birthday meal, but Libra, Aquarius and Pisces are all attracted by the prospect of this sparkling stimulant. It may well be that champagne does something for those born under these signs and for them it is even of mildly medicinal value.

Some physicians still insist that the therapeutic properties of champagne are considerable. However, this applies to a good vintage champagne which, some say, is a valuable aid to those suffering from depression, dyspepsia, gout, influenza and neuralgia. Both Byron and Dickens suffered from fits of depression and both paid tribute to the restorative qualities of champagne. It is little wonder that Byron went so far as to declare that "the best of life is but intoxication", even if this is a most unwise precept to follow.

There is a lot of trendy nonsense talked (and, alas, written) about which wines should be drunk with certain dishes. What is important to observe is not so much the normally accepted rules, but what constitutes individual taste. A recent symposium of six French gastronomic critics proved that even the experts cannot always agree on which wine goes with which dish.

These wine critics were asked by a weekly news magazine, *Le Point*, to name the appropriate wine for a variety of dishes. Their answer ranged from port to champagne. Rarely was there full agreement. For example, they were asked what they would drink with *foie gras* (fatted goose liver). Four picked a white wine and, surprisingly, three of them opted for a sauterne (a sweet wine). Of the other two one chose champagne and the other, most unconventionally, picked a port. With pheasant and other game they all agreed a red wine was essential, but their choice ranged widely from a light claret to a full-bodied wine from the Auvergne.

So it is not a bad idea to ascertain beforehand if your guest to be has any such quirks. I do stress *guest*, not guests: you can cater for the foibles of one, or two at a pinch, beyond that it becomes either impossible, or ridiculously expensive.

There are certain basic rules to which you should adhere. You must
ave white wines with fish and red wines for beef, mutton and game.
owever, there is a fairly extensive "middle ground", including
icken, white meats such as veal and turkey, of course, in which
ther red or white can be drunk according to individual tastes. But
is normally a safe rule that white meats and chicken call for a white
ine.

You will find that on the whole people tend to be fussier about
hite wines than they are about red. Some cannot stand a sweet white
d only like one that is very dry indeed. You should always remember
hen buying white wine that a medium dry white is not far short of
eing a sweet wine.

To acquire a really detailed knowledge of wines and vintages takes
ears of experience and sampling. Few people can claim to have this
nowledge unless they are either in the wine trade, or have a large
urse and the leisure in which to indulge it. Most top vintage wines
day – I am thinking of the really good years such as 1949 and 1959
are priced so high that one can only buy them on very special
ccasions and then only for someone who really does appreciate the
ifference.

But this is no excuse for not having a shot at gleaning some basic
nderstanding of what Hilaire Belloc called, "Wine, privilege of the
ompletely free".

If you are serving any white wine, champagne included, either put
in an ice-bucket before serving, or pop the bottle into the refrigerator
t least an hour beforehand. Similarly, insist on getting the same
ind of service at a restaurant, if you are giving a birthday meal
ere.

All red wines should be given the opportunity to "breathe" – i.e. to
ave the cork removed from the bottle – half an hour before serving.
his is also true of white wines, which is why an ice-bucket is more
ensible than a refrigerator, but possibly much less so. Despite what
urists may say, it is not quite so vital to warm the bottle of red as it
to cool the bottle of white. But much depends on the time of year.
t is certainly ill-advised to serve red wine which has been kept in a
ery cool place in the middle of a cold winter without warming it
rst. It is desirable that all reds should at least be at "room temper-
ture" for an hour before serving. Remember, if your bottle has been
a very cold place, it will take much longer to warm up and you may
eed to keep it propped against the central heating.

You will be told by horrified purists that it is an act of vinous blasphemy to warm up your bottle of red wine by plunging it into hot water. Frankly, whatever the experts may say, this is little more than a piece of snobbism. If you need to warm a very cold bottle of red wine quickly – say within a quarter of an hour – I would say to hell with the experts and just leave it standing in a sinkfull of very hot, but not boiling water. It is much better than serving it chilled. Watch that you don't lose the label in the process. Alternatively, you could decant the wine afterwards.

These are all fairly obvious tips to most of you, but I cite them because out of every six obvious rules one may cite, there is nearly always one that has previously been missed by all of us. For example, if you are giving a meal at home, it is a sound plan to taste some of the wine before serving it. Obvious? Yes, but how many of us always do this? If you have struck unlucky by any chance, you will still have time to rectify the error. There is much more bad wine about today than was ever the case before. This applies especially to those "bargains" (?) announced by the supermarkets.

In the birthday menus suggested in this book I have omitted a cheese course for two reasons: first, many people find 3 courses ample, and, secondly, cheese is very much a matter of individual taste. It is nearly always best to allow for cheese as an optional course, whether at home or at a restaurant. If the latter, it need not be ordered beforehand and presents no problem if somebody suddenly wants it. But it is wise, when serving a meal at home, to have a selection of cheeses available in case someone opts for that either instead of a sweet, or in addition to it.

I would suggest that you always keep in reserve a choice of at least three cheeses for such an emergency, bearing in mind that while some adore Camembert and Gorgonzola, others much prefer the milder Wensleydale, Cheshire or Caerphilly. Don't waste a superior and costly wine on cheese since, curiously enough, cheese has the quality of making even an *ordinaire* wine taste better than average. But you should see there is some red wine left for your compulsive cheese-eater. If there has been no red wine for the dinner, then offer a glass of port, or, have a half bottle of red wine handy. A small carafe of red would do admirably.

The buying of wines must inevitably depend on the money you have available. It is possible to get some excellent bargains at supermarkets (an excellent example has been the Goldener Oktober moselle, which is good by most standards), but you can make some disastrous purchases. By far the best policy is to try out one bottle at a time and then, when you have made a find like, say, Goldener Oktober, buy a further half dozen or dozen for stocking up. But it is safest to be guided by a reliable wine merchant, even if you have to pay that much more. On the other hand, whisky, gin, brandy, rum, sherry, Dubonnet and some liqueurs you can safely buy at the supermarkets.

You will probably win a better reputation with your friends and be on safer ground if you stick mainly to French wines, preferably choosing those which are bottled in France. You have a wider range of wines, both white and red, rosé and sparkling, in France than in any other country in the world.

You need to acquire more detailed knowledge before venturing too much into other territories. But it isn't a bad idea to decide which other country's wines you like and then to set out to study their lists, sample them and gradually to become an authority in a modest way on that other nation's wines.

Be very careful with Italian wines, avoiding the cheapest and those with doubtful labels – especially the *ordinaires* or carafes – as in the last 20 years a good deal of bogus and doctored wine has been exported from Italy through illicit channels. Many Italian wines do not travel well, though the producers seem to have overcome this rather better in recent years. Red Chianti and Lacrimae Christi (a splendid golden white) are both apt to be bad travellers. Recently some splendid Sicilian wines, especially their white, have come on the market.

Rosé at its best is a refreshing and pleasant wine, though often scorned by connoisseurs. Again, you are safer with the many French rosés – their Anjou Rosé is bottled by several British firms – but there are both Portuguese and Spanish wines of this type. It pays to buy a rosé in the higher price range.

Spain has some excellent wines, but except for their sherries, they are not extensively exported. Supermarket Spanish wine tends to be over-sweet and of poor value, though unquestionably cheap. But if you want a reliable Spanish red, you can't do better than look around for a Marques de Riscal; for a white, a good choice would be Diamante.

As to Hocks and Rieslings, the German are best and safest, but some Yugoslav wines of this type are quite passable. Some Swiss wines are excellent value, but you will not so easily find them.

I have tried to select liqueurs which will appeal to all signs, but this is not always an easy task. Some of those I have listed are not obtainable at all wine merchants, for example, *Parfait d'Amour,* the purple coloured liqueur chosen for sweet-toothed Libra. This liqueur has an *ambience* of its own admirably suited to romance-loving Libra.

It is not a bad idea to lay in a stock of liqueur miniatures, or, failing that, quarter bottles, so that you always have a fair selection to fall back on.

But you may find that most men prefer brandy to a liqueur, or at least a liqueur brandy. It is worth noting that the smooth Armagnac is more suitable for women guests, while some men prefer the fiery Spanish Pedro Domecq brandy, or a Rémy-Martin. Some of you may be puzzled by the V.S.O.P. on cognac (brandy from the Cognac area of France) bottles. It simply means "Very Superior Old Pale", which may surprise you, but it is a tribute to the close links between France and Britain in the brandy trade.

There is, however, a French version of V.S.O.P., which has been taken up by Rémy-Martin more in jest than anything else: it is *"versez sans oublier personne"*, which means "pour without forgetting anyone!"

I have included some recipes which require wine as an ingredient. It is always as well to keep in stock the odd bottle of a cheap white or a cheap red wine solely for cooking. I have stressed cheap, not cheap and nasty, or a wine that is too sweet, too acid or with a bitter tang. Remember when it comes to cooking with wine, you and you alone must be the arbiter. One can give a recipe, but one cannot stipulate exactly how much wine you should use. The person doing the cooking must decide that by tasting and tasting again and again, if necessary. If you feel that where I have stated one tablespoon of wine, two would be better, so be it. You cook with wine by trial and error.

When cooking with white wine, choose as dry a wine as possible. With red wine you don't have to lay down any special rules. For sweets Madeira and Marsala are rather better than sherry, but if you should substitute sherry, ensure that it is a dark, sweet sherry.

When cooking fish with wine, remember that draught cider makes a good substitute for white wine.

The home-made brewer of wine will find that the gypsies have a certain amount of astrological lore in their recipes for the do-it-yourself drinker. But this is really a separate subject and requires lengthy study. But perhaps it will not come amiss to wind up this appendix on drinking around the zodiac with the following sub-heading:

How to drink, keep fit and still be loved

For certain signs of the zodiac brandy is definitely a drink to avoid. This goes for Gemini and Taurus, and, though we have allowed Leo a Courvoisier brandy in his birthday menu (for Leo loves brandy), Leonians, because of their tendency towards heart trouble in middle age, should lay off brandy altogether as they get older.

It is a little known fact that brandy (contrary to popular belief) is not good for heart cases or for diaphragmatic hernia. Malt whisky is far better than brandy for the heart case.

Champagne has proved to be an excellent stimulant in an illness, when no other stimulant can be retained by the patient. Elixir, a liqueur made both in Belgium and the Pyrenees, is a cure both for indigestion and acute stomach ache. Its full name is Elixir de Spa, as it is principally made in the town of Spa. Fernet Branca is still far and away the best cure for a hang-over or feelings of acute nausea. A small bottle kept in your wine cupboard is a wise precaution.

This book is nevertheless intended for the cook, not the drinker, but a good cook should know quite a lot about drinks. To wind up, here is a brief table of suggestions for the choice of wines and drinks for a meal:

For aperitifs: Dry sherry (La Ina or Tio Pepe); Dubonnet; St. Raphael; gin and tonic; dry Martini; or even a chilled white wine (say, a Moselle).

With hors d'oeurves: Chablis, Graves, Moselle, or any dry white wine.

With fish: positively white wine: Chablis, Hock, Riesling, Champagne.

With red meat and game: Red wine: Chateau Neuf du Pape, St. Emilion, Beaujolais, Chianti (red); Marques de Riscal.

With sweets: A sweet goes better with a white wine than with a red, just as cheese goes better with a red than a white. A sweet wine goes well with the pudding course – a Sauterne, or a sweet Moselle.

Liqueurs served with fruit: strawberries can be effectively laced with Kirsch or Cointreau; cherries with brandy; oranges with rum and Curacoa.

For your kitchen and medicine chest

Appended is a quick reference list of points to bear in mind for health and cooking purposes for each sign of the zodiac. This will be useful both for your friends and yourself:

Aries
Health: Nerves cause quick temper and frequent irritation. Eye-strain needs to be guarded against and eyes should be tested regularly. Prone to headaches, stomach and kidney ailments.
Birth salt: Phosphate of potassium (this can be taken in tablet form, but a prescription should be obtained).
Beneficial foods: Apples, celery, grapefruit, cauliflower, cabbage, spinach, lemons, lettuce, carrots, beetroot, tomatoes and dates.
Beneficial herbs: Broom, valerian and hops.

Taurus
Health: Liver ailments in later life, and a watch needs to be kept on the nose and throat. Throat and neck are weak points in Taurus. Some tendency to rheumatism.
Birth salt: Sulphate of soda (this can also be taken in tablet form – *natrum sulphuricum*).
Beneficial foods: Apples, celery, lettuce, spinach, kale, radishes prunes, blackberries, strawberries, honey and asparagus.

Beneficial herbs: Coltsfoot (the leaves of this herb when brewed make a refreshing drink and cure for colds, or you can make coltsfoot wine) and mint. Mint tea is particularly good for Taurians.

Gemini

Health: Geminians need to guard against eyestrain and nervous ailments. They are apt to overdo things and bring on nervous exhaustion and sometimes nervous breakdowns. Catarrh and constipation are minor ills to which they are prone.
Birth salt: Potassium Chloride (this can also be taken in tablet form)
Beneficial foods: Apples, celery, grapefruit, green beans, cauliflower,. cabbage, kale, lettuce, watercress, pineapple, spinach, carrots, tomatoes.
Beneficial Herbs: aniseed, caraway, red clover and valerian.

Cancer

Health: Digestive troubles are likely to be experienced by Cancerians unless care is taken with their diet. The stomach and the liver are their weakest points and sometimes they are subject to nervous strain.
Birth salt: Calcium fluoride (this again can be taken in tablet form).
Beneficial foods: cabbage (both green and red), kale, watercress, milk, cottage cheese, prunes, onions, parsley, raisins, oranges, lemons, leeks, rye bread, mushrooms, turnips and cucumber.
Beneficial herbs: Wintergreen, witch hazel.

Leo

Health: Leonians are remarkably healthy and long-lived as a general rule and have few health worries. However, they need to guard against overtaxing the heart, especially in middle age. There is also a tendency towards back troubles and poor circulation. They are apt to put too great a strain on themselves and always need more rest than they imagine to be necessary.
Birth salt: Magnesium phosphate (can be taken in tablet form).
Beneficial foods: Almonds, citrus, cabbage, plums, honey, bran, rice, peas, sugar beet, oranges, lettuce, walnuts.
Beneficial herbs: Celandine, dill, nettles (used as a vegetable, valuable as a blood purifier and also an antidote to rheumatism as it gets rid of uric acid), St. John's wort, fennel, parsley and mint.

Virgo

Health: Most of the Virgoan's health worries are minor ones, concerning the stomach, the throat and the nervous system. This all tends to make them more hypochrondiac than most people, though that may be too strong a term to apply to most Virgoans. But let us say they tend to worry about their health, often without telling anyone else. Diet needs watching, especially as they love good food.

Birth Salt: Potassium sulphate (this can be taken in tablet form and should be so consumed to stave off recurring colds, catarrh and sore throats).

Beneficial Foods: Apples, celery, grapefruit, cauliflower, cabbage, spinach, lemons, carrots, tomatoes dates, cucumber and beetroot.

Beneficial Herbs: There are a number of herbs which contain potassium sulphate – rosemary, valerian, poke root. Other worthwhile herbs for this sign of the zodiac are caraway, starwort and cornflower.

Libra

Health: Kidney trouble is the most prevalent ailment with Librans. Otherwise, except for a tendency to nervous exhaustion with backache and, in a few cases, diabetes, they are a healthy, life-loving lot.

Birth Salt: Sodium phosphate (can be taken in tablet form).

Beneficial Foods: apples, asparagus, celery, green beans, lettuce, grapes, almonds, spinach, kale, radishes, prunes, blackberries, strawberries, honey.

Beneficial Herbs: Dandelion (especially good for the kidneys and full of vitamin A and vitamin C), celery tops (more a vegetable than a herb, but can be used as a herbal tonic), cloves, figwort.

Scorpio

Health: Scorpio's temperament encourages sudden bursts of energy followed by intermittent periods of lying low and resting. The Scorpion needs to balance up these different periods so that there are fairly frequent short rest periods and not too long spent using up all one's energy. They are sometimes prone to abscesses, boils, ulcers and catarrh. Their generative organs need watchfulness, both as regards male and female, these sometimes being weak points.

Birth Salt: Calcium sulphate (can be taken in tablet form and is good for warding off trouble with boils, ulcers and sometimes even abscesses).

Beneficial Foods: Cabbage (both green and red), kale, watercress, milk, cottage cheese, prunes, onions, parsley, raisins, oranges, lemons, leeks, rye bread, mushrooms, turnips and cucumber.

Beneficial Herbs: Witch hazel, horseradish, marigold, sarsaparilla.

Sagittarius

Health: Sagittarians, being lovers of the outdoors life and of sport, are prone to accidents. Statistics by doctors show that these accidents usually occur to the hips, thighs and similar joints. Hips and thighs are weak points with Sagittarians, not only for accidents, but for rheumatism in later life. Blood disorders, nervous exhaustion and minor ailments of hair and nails are other ills to which the otherwise healthy Sagittarian is prone.

Birth Salt: Silica (this can be taken in tablet form. It can be recommended especially for such minor ills as fungi on fingernails and toenails and lustreless, receding hair).

Beneficial Foods: Asparagus, cucumber, parsnips, Scotch oats, strawberries, onions, wheat, cherries, rye, barley, red cabbage, black figs, tomatoes.

Beneficial Herbs: Marjoram, chicory, agrimony, dandelion, balsam, sage and borage.

Capricorn

Health: Capricornians' weak points tend to be the liver, knees and teeth – in that order. Some, unless they watch their diet, are subject to intestinal ailments and rheumatism. On the whole they are very healthy, but as they get older they need to watch their lungs and avoid the probability of recurring colds.

Birth Salt: Calcium phosphate (can be taken in tablet form).

Beneficial Foods: Cabbage (both green and red), kale, watercress, milk, cottage cheese, prunes, onions, parsley, raisins, oranges, lemons, leeks, rye bread, mushrooms, turnips and cucumber.

Beneficial Herbs: Aconite, comfrey, plantain, heartsease, malt and elder.

Aquarius

Health: For Aquarians the nervous system, legs and ankles are the usual source of trouble. There is a link between the nervous system and the digestive system which in Aquarius can be a constant source of trouble, so diet needs to be watched. They often prove to be extremely good – sometimes better than their doctors – at diagnosing their own ailments and, more important, how to cure them. Their circulation may give them some concern.

Birth Salt: Sodium chloride (this is the equivalent of common table salt, but it would be wrong to think that any deficiency in this birth salt could be compensated for by just taking table salt. It can be taken in tablet form – Natrum Muriaticum – or through the recommended foods and herbs. If excessive doses of table salt are taken this could cause hardening of the arteries and skin diseases.)

Beneficial Foods: Apples, celery, lettuce, spinach, kale, radishes, prunes, pears, blackberries, strawberries, honey, asparagus and grapes.

Beneficial Herbs: Coltsfoot, marshmallow, sorrel, tansy and valerian.

Pisces

Health: Pisceans suffer from a number of ailments consequent upon a deficiency in their birth salt – palpitations of the heart, rheumatism, insomnia, headaches, nervous upsets. Their weak point is their ankles and feet and, to a lesser extent, their legs.

Birth Salt: Iron phosphate (which can also be taken in tablet form). This is enormously important for checking their tendency to the ailments mentioned.

Beneficial Foods: A varied range of foods is especially beneficial to Pisceans – dried fruits such as raisins, dates, figs, prunes and apricots, green beans, broccoli, spinach, lettuce, peas (both fresh and dried), all root vegetables, most fresh fruit, nuts and bran.

Beneficial Herbs: Saxifrage, camomile, peppermint, vervain.

Postscript

It was in the last century that German doctors first linked our state of health with the twelve tissue salts (birth salts) found in a healthy body. Their experiments showed that a deficiency or imbalance of one or more salts leads to various ailments and diseases. This could be remedied by taking minute doses of the missing salts. It was later that there was an astrological – homeopathic link-up on this discovery and that the individual came to be regarded as needing individual treatment and not just treatment by the rules of medical science. Each of the birth salts can be obtained through health food stores or by prescription from a homeopathic doctor. These salts are quite harmless and can be used for self-treatment following advice, preferably from a homeopathic doctor. You can obtain further details of homeopathic treatment from the Royal London Homeopathic Hospital, Great Ormond Street, London WC 1, or the British Homeopathic Association, 24 Dorset Square, London NW 1.

Index